# Bond

# Verbal Reasoning

## Assessment Papers

**9–10 years**
**Book 1**

**J M Bond**
**Frances Down**

Great Clarendon Street, Oxford, OX2 6DP, United Kingdom

Oxford University Press is a department of the University of Oxford. It furthers the University's objective of excellence in research, scholarship, and education by publishing worldwide. Oxford is a registered trade mark of Oxford University Press in the UK and in certain other countries



First published in 2003 by Nelson Thornes Ltd
This edition published in 2014



British Library Cataloguing in Publication Data
Data available

978-1-4085-2517-3

10 9 8 7 6 5 4 3

Printed in Great Britain

Page make-up by OKS Prepress, India

# Before you get started

## What is Bond?

This book is part of the Bond Assessment Papers series for verbal reasoning, which provides a **thorough and progressive course in verbal reasoning** from ages six to twelve. It builds up reasoning skills from book to book over the course of the series.

## What does this book cover and how can it be used to prepare for exams?

Verbal reasoning questions can be grouped into four distinct groups: sorting words, selecting words, anagrams, coded sequences and logic. *Verbal Reasoning 9–10 Book 1 and Book 2* practise a wide range of questions appropriate to the age group drawn from all these categories. The papers can be used both for general practice and as part of the run-up to 11+ and other selective exams. One of the key features of Bond Assessment Papers is that each one practises **a very wide variety of skills and question types** so that children are always challenged to think – and don't get bored repeating the same question type again and again. We believe that variety is the key to effective learning. It helps children 'think on their feet' and cope with the unexpected: it is surprising how often children come out of verbal reasoning exams having met question types they have not seen before.

## What does this book contain?

- **15 papers** – each one contains 65 questions.
- **Tutorial links throughout** – – this icon appears in the margin next to the questions. It indicates links to the relevant section in *How to do ... 11+ Verbal Reasoning*, our invaluable subject guide that offers explanations and practice for all core question types.
- **Scoring devices** – there are score boxes in the margins and a Progress Chart on page 60. The chart is a visual and motivating way for children to see how they are doing. It also turns the score into a percentage that can help decide what to do next.
- **Next Steps Planner** – advice on what to do after finishing the papers can be found on the inside back cover.
- **Answers** – located in an easily-removed central pull-out section.

## How can you use this book?

One of the great strengths of Bond Assessment Papers is their flexibility. They can be used at home, in school and by tutors to:

- set **timed formal practice** tests – allow about 40 minutes per paper. Reduce the suggested time limit by five minutes to practise working at speed.
- provide **bite-sized chunks** for regular practice
- **highlight strengths and weaknesses** in the core skills
- identify **individual needs**
- set **homework**
- follow a **complete 11+ preparation strategy** alongside *The Parents' Guide to the 11+* (see overleaf).

It is best to start at the beginning and work though the papers in order. If you are using the book as part of a careful run-in to the 11+, we suggest that you also have two other essential Bond resources close at hand:

*How to do ... 11+ Verbal Reasoning*: the subject guide that explains all the question types practised in this book. Use the cross-reference icons to find the relevant sections.

*The Parents' Guide to the 11+*: the step-by-step guide to the whole 11+ experience. It clearly explains the 11+ process, provides guidance on how to assess children, helps you to set complete action plans for practice and explains how you can use *Verbal Reasoning 9–10 Book 1 and Book 2* as part of a strategic run-in to the exam.

See the inside front cover for more details of these books.

## What does a score mean and how can it be improved?

It is unfortunately impossible to predict how a child will perform when it comes to the 11+ (or similar) exam if they achieve a certain score on any practice book or paper. Success on the day depends on a host of factors, including the scores of the other children sitting the test. However, we can give some guidance on what a score indicates and how to improve it.

If children colour in the Progress Chart on page 60, this will give an idea of present performance in percentage terms. The Next Steps Planner inside the back cover will help you to decide what to do next to help a child progress. It is always valuable to go over wrong answers with children. If they are having trouble with any particular question type, follow the tutorial links to *How to do ... 11+ Verbal Reasoning* for step-by-step explanations and further practice.

## *Don't forget the website...!*

Visit www.bond11plus.co.uk for lots of advice, information and suggestions on everything to do with Bond, the 11+ and helping children to do their best, and exams.

# Paper 1

Underline the pair of words most similar in meaning.

**Example** come, go <u>roam, wander</u> fear, fare

1 fly, wing easy, simple under, over

2 go, depart quarrel, agree write, read

3 narrow, broad plain, decorated new, fresh

4 night, day collect, distribute tired, weary

5 hide, conceal rush, delay jump, walk

Underline the two words, one from each group, which are most opposite in meaning.

**Example** (dawn, <u>early</u>, wake) (<u>late</u>, stop, sunrise)

6 (sell, make, use) (study, purchase, remove)

7 (dim, weak, sturdy) (bright, mild, blurry)

8 (long, far, back) (distance, front, length)

9 (lesson, question, talk) (report, teacher, answer)

10 (accept, advance, aware) (refuse, alive, rubbish)

Complete the following sentences by selecting the most sensible word from each group of words given in the brackets. Underline the words selected.

**Example** The (<u>children</u>, books, foxes) carried the (houses, <u>books</u>, steps) home from the (greengrocer, <u>library</u>, factory).

11 The (farmer, sailor, boy) was going to the (docks, shed, swimming pool) to (shop, milk the cows, read a book).

12 Ann took her (spoon, spade, hoe) to the (garden, beach, park) as she wanted to build a (bridge, castle, palace).

13 Don't (put, lose, forget) to (find, eat, post) this (stamp, sock, letter).

14 The (plane, porter, eagle) carried the (sea, suitcase, food) to its (runway, nest, ground).

15 The (television, friend, lantern) lit his (face, knee, elbow), as he (ran, threw, buried) the treasure.

Underline the two words which are made from the same letters.

**Example** TAP PET <u>TEA</u> POT <u>EAT</u>

16 PIANO PLATE PLAYS PEDAL PETAL

17 SHALL HOUSE SHORE HOMES HORSE

| | | | | | |
|---|---|---|---|---|---|
| **18** | CHAIR | CHEST | TABLE | BLAME | BLEAT |
| **19** | BEACH | BENCH | BOUGH | HEADS | SHADE |
| **20** | LEAST | PLEAT | LATER | STALE | TABLE |

5

Write the four-letter word hidden at the end of one word and the beginning of the next word. The order of the letters may not be changed.

B 21

**Example** The children had bats and balls. sand

**21** This book can be very useful. ________

**22** The rough lad was very strong. ________

**23** There are fairies at the bottom of the garden. ________

**24** This house is often cold. ________

**25** Will the journey end soon? ________

5

Find the letter which will end the first word and start the second word.

B 10

**Example** peac ( h ) ome

**26** mad ( __ ) rror **27** ris ( __ ) ing **28** lis ( __ ) hen

**29** til ( __ ) eave **30** foo ( __ ) rade

5

Find and underline the two words which need to change places for each sentence to make sense.

B 17

**Example** She went to letter the write.

**31** How do you today feel?

**32** As tights is cold I am wearing it.

**33** I like hairdo new your.

**34** I'm sorry glass broken the I've.

**35** I'll home to get him have.

5

Fill in the missing letters and numbers. The alphabet has been written out to help you.

B 23

**Example** AB is to CD as PQ is to RS .

A B C D E F G H I J K L M N O P Q R S T U V W X Y Z

**36** AB is to CD as EF is to ________.

**37** AC is to DF as GI is to ________.

**38** M2 is to N4 as O6 is to ________.

**39** 9BC is to 12BC as 15BC is to ________.

**40** 8AB is to 6BC as 4CD is to ________.

5

Which one letter can be added to the front of all of these words to make new words?

B 12

**Example** c̲are c̲at c̲rate c̲all

41 __ate __ear __our __ist

42 __harp __lender __hut __lit

43 __edge __asp __allow __hole

44 __ace __aid __age __ale

45 __ate __ream __angle __rove

5

Fill in the crosswords so that all the given words are included. You have been given one letter as a clue in each crossword.

B 19

46

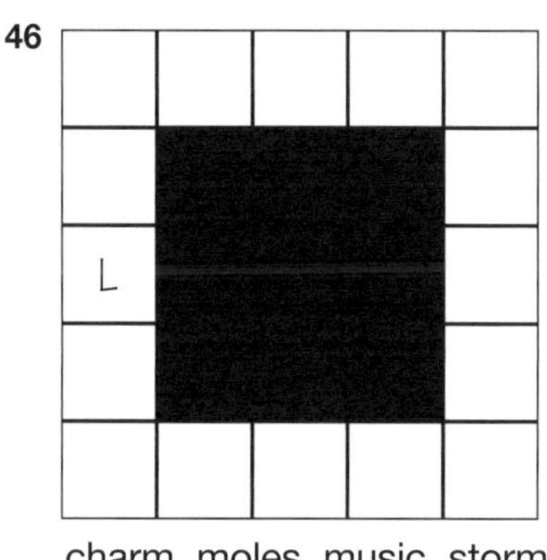


charm, moles, music, storm

47

I

heart, humps, stalk, trick

48

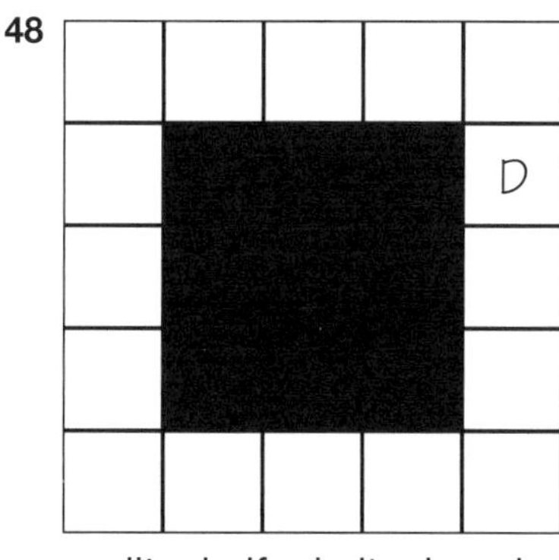


edits, knife, knits, knock

49

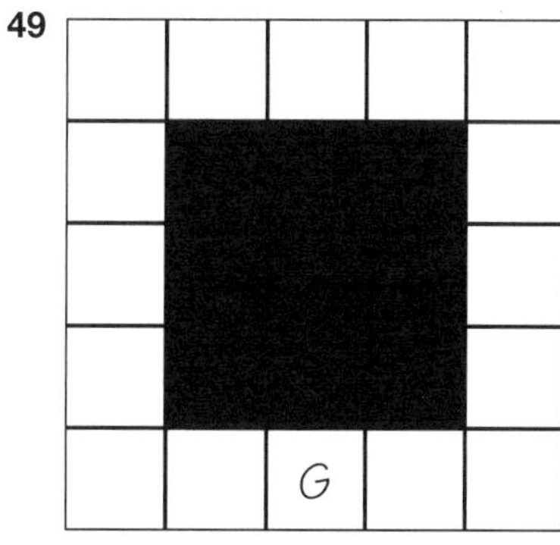


films, finer, fluff, rages

50

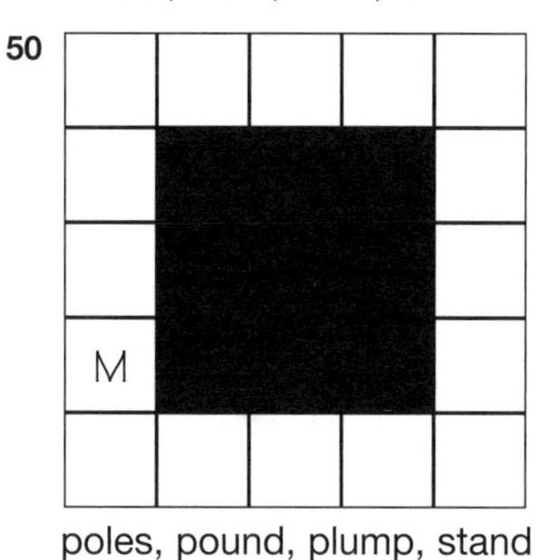


poles, pound, plump, stand

5

If the code for PROTECT is £ ! : * ? / *, what are the codes for the following words?

**51** TORE ________ **52** PORT ________ **53** CROP ________

B 24

3

If the code for PLANTER is ÷ = + : − % ×, what do the following codes stand for?

**54** −×+÷ ________ **55** ×%+= ________

B 24

2

Choose the word or phrase that makes each sentence true.

B 14

**Example** A LIBRARY always has (posters, a carpet, books, DVDs, stairs).

**56** A BIRD always has a (nest, beak, chick, worm, twig).

**57** A PLANT always has (flowers, berries, roots, branches, a pot).

**58** A SHOE always has a (strap, button, sole, zipper, foot).

**59** A HOUSE always has (bricks, walls, a drive, a garden, a doorbell).

**60** A COAT always has (buttons, pockets, sleeves, a belt, a zipper).

5

Remove two letters from the word in capital letters to leave a new word. The meaning of the new word is given in the clue.

B 12

**Example** MONKEY lives in a monastery monk

**61** STREET type of plant ________

**62** LEARNT tilt ________

**63** STRAND on a beach ________

**64** FRAMES renown ________

**65** SPRAIN twirl ________

5

***Now go to the Progress Chart to record your score!*** **Total** 65

# Paper 2

Underline the two words in each line which are most similar in type or meaning.

**Example** dear pleasant poor extravagant expensive

| | | | | |
|---|---|---|---|---|
| **1** alter | after | sound | fond | change |
| **2** form | frozen | fear | fell | fright |
| **3** sit | fidget | stand | wriggle | kick |
| **4** ready | right | hard | simple | difficult |
| **5** start | end | lend | begin | borrow |

5

Underline the pair of words most opposite in meaning.

**Example** cup, mug coffee, milk hot, cold

| | | |
|---|---|---|
| **6** circle, round | shiny, dull | enemy, foe |
| **7** pause, rest | generous, mean | angry, cross |
| **8** home, away | bridge, river | yours, his |
| **9** often, seldom | great, big | speak, talk |
| **10** tug, pull | raise, lower | push, shove |

Underline two words, one from each group, that go together to form a new word. The word in the first group always comes first.

**Example** (hand, green, for) (light, house, sure)

| | |
|---|---|
| **11** (name, pay, try) | (less, use, more) |
| **12** (keep, look, out) | (safe, sane, sake) |
| **13** (on, be, in) | (head, wind, shoulders) |
| **14** (chapter, page, text) | (book, mark, word) |
| **15** (cub, key, money) | (board, lock, safe) |

Find the three-letter word which can be added to the letters in capitals to make a new word. The new word will complete the sentence sensibly.

**Example** The cat sprang onto the MO. USE

**16** The thief was arrested for SLING a car. ________

**17** The grandmother thought that the children had GN quite a bit since she'd last seen them. ________

**18** The class went to the THRE to see a pantomime. ________

**19** Dad WED the food up in the oven because we were late for lunch. ________

**20** The woman put the flowers she had just picked in a BET. ________

5

Write the four-letter word hidden at the end of one word and the beginning of the next word. The order of the letters may not be changed.

**Example** The children had bats and balls. sand

21 This candle is very pretty. ________

22 You must learn the alphabet. ________

23 My grandmother bakes delicious cakes. ________

24 The strong wind took the kite miles away. ________

25 He drove the car in the mud. ________

Change the first word into the last word, by changing one letter at a time and making a new, different word in the middle.

**Example** CASE CASH LASH

26 SEND ________ SANG

27 CAKE ________ MALE

28 DEAR ________ MEAL

29 CALL ________ BAIL

30 HOME ________ COMB

Complete the following sentences by selecting the most sensible word from each group of words given in the brackets. Underline the words selected.

**Example** The (children, books, foxes) carried the (houses, books, steps) home from the (greengrocer, library, factory).

31 The (sheep, lions, dogs) were in a (town, field, shop) grazing the (bones, grass, chicken) contentedly.

32 The (dog, otter, tiger) paced back and forth in the (jungle, cage, field) at the (farm, zoo, park).

33 Under a (stone, book, kitchen) there lived a (house, pond, frog) who ate (dogs, porridge, flies).

34 The (new, fast, old) car crept slowly (through, along, up) the (sunny, flat, steep) hill.

35 Don't (swim, eat, move)! There's a (pig, coat, snake) on that (shelf, sun, rock).

Choose two words, one from each set of brackets, to complete the sentences in the best way.

**Example** Smile is to happiness as (drink, tear, shout) is to (whisper, laugh, sorrow).

36 Tuesday is to Wednesday as (May, March, April) is to (March, May, July).

37 Puppy is to dog as (cat, lamb, ewe) is to (dog, sheep, pig).

38 Author is to book as (man, sculptor, artist) is to (picture, paint, woman).

39 Plate is to eat as (knife, cup, watch) is to (drink, fork, saucer).

40 Aunt is to niece as (mother, uncle, nephew) is to (nephew, boy, sister).

Fill in the crosswords so that all the given words are included. You have been given one letter as a clue in each crossword.

41

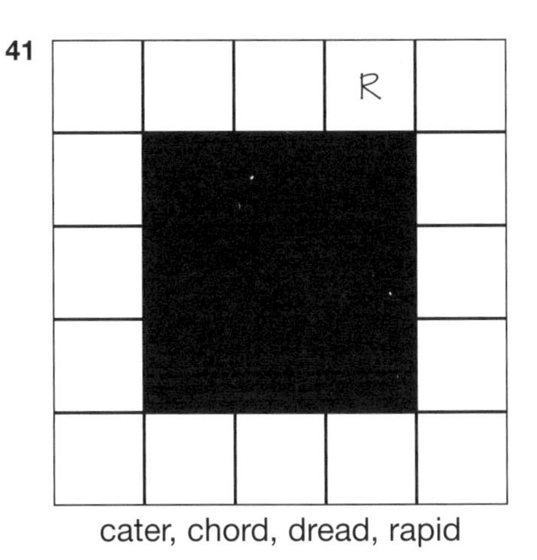


cater, chord, dread, rapid

42

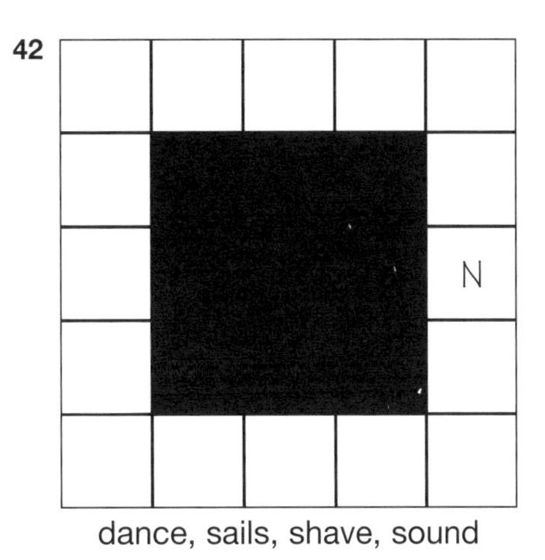


dance, sails, shave, sound

43

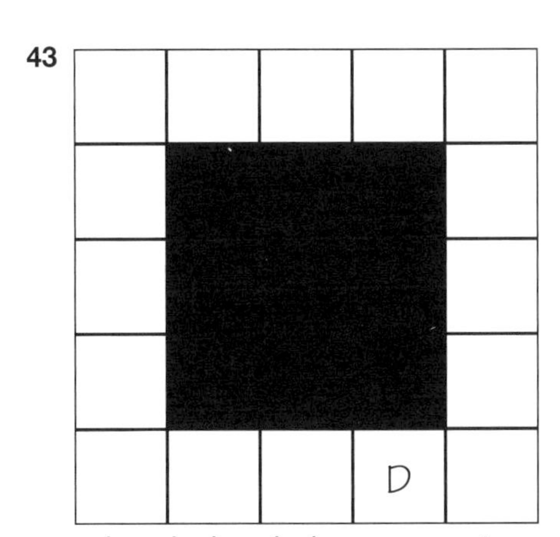


handy, harsh, human, nasty

44

curse, eases, ropes, taper

45

camps, mouth, other, truce

5

Give the missing numbers in the following sequences.

B 23

| | | | | | | |
|---|---|---|---|---|---|---|
| **Example** | 2 | 4 | 6 | 8 | 10 | 12 |
| **46** | 91 | ___ | 73 | 64 | ___ | 46 |
| **47** | ___ | $\frac{3}{4}$ | ___ | $1\frac{1}{4}$ | $1\frac{1}{2}$ | $1\frac{3}{4}$ |
| **48** | 70 | ___ | ___ | 49 | 42 | 35 |
| **49** | 66 | 77 | 88 | ___ | ___ | 121 |
| **50** | 1 | 2 | 4 | 5 | ___ | ___ |

5

Here are the codes for four words. Match the right word to the right code.

B 24

| MAN | AND | MEN | AN |
|---|---|---|---|
| ❍ ■ ❞ | ❍ △ ❞ | △ ❞ | △ ❞ ◆ |

**51** MAN ____________ **52** AND ____________

**53** MEN ____________ **54** AN ____________

**55** Using the same code, encode MEND. ____________

5

Find the letter which will complete both pairs of words, ending the first word and starting the second. The same letter must be used for both pairs of words.

B 10

**Example** mea ( t ) able fi ( t ) ub

**56** lim ( ___ ) ars ru ( ___ ) oy

**57** pai ( ___ ) one tal ( ___ ) og

**58** mad ( ___ ) very tir ( ___ ) nd

**59** tha ( ___ ) ry se ( ___ ) one

**60** son ( ___ ) rim le ( ___ ) ap

5

Rearrange the letters in capitals to make another word. The new word has something to do with the first two words.

B 16

| | | | | |
|---|---|---|---|---|
| **Example** | spot | soil | SAINT | STAIN |
| **61** | pain | throb | EACH | ____________ |
| **62** | start | commence | BEING | ____________ |
| **63** | beneath | lower | ELBOW | ____________ |
| **64** | inexpensive | economical | PEACH | ____________ |
| **65** | man | boy | MEAL | ____________ |

5

***Now go to the Progress Chart to record your score!*** **Total** 65

# Paper 3

Underline the word in the brackets that goes best with the words given outside the brackets.

B 5

**Example** word, paragraph, sentence (pen, cap, letter, top, stop)

1 sleet, snow, rain (sunny, hot, frost, cool, hail)

2 sty, lair, hutch (flat, bungalow, hotel, cottage, stable)

3 sprouts, beans, swede (oranges, plums, blackberries, carrots, limes)

4 talk, chatter, utter (cough, speak, blow, splutter, sneeze)

5 children, tots, infants (age, school, toddlers, adults, grannies)

5

Underline the two words, one from each group, which are the most opposite in meaning.

B 9

**Example** (dawn, early, wake) (late, stop, sunrise)

6 (money, spend, purse) (cash, notes, save)

7 (equal, same, mend) (similar, different, cheap)

8 (join, quit, try) (wait, start, consider)

9 (crowded, alone, lonely) (deserted, earned, bought)

10 (wrestle, fight, hurt) (heal, war, wrong)

5

Find the letter which will end the first word and start the second word.

B 10

**Example** peac ( h ) ome

11 tim ( ___ ) ast

12 sea ( ___ ) ray

13 men ( ___ ) iet

14 spea ( ___ ) est

15 bal ( ___ ) and

5

Find a word that can be put in front of each of the following words to make new, compound words.

B 11

| | | | | |
|---|---|---|---|---|
| **Example** cast | fall | ward | pour | down |
| 16 ball | step | print | path | ________ |
| 17 stairs | set | right | turn | ________ |
| 18 mark | shelf | keeper | worm | ________ |
| 19 side | form | hale | put | ________ |
| 20 scarf | lock | light | quarters | ________ |

5

Write the four-letter word hidden at the end of one word and the beginning of the next word. The order of the letters may not be changed.

B 21

**Example** The children had bats and balls. sand

21 These curtains are too long. ________

22 The time shows it is quite late. ________

23 I like the sea and the mountains. ________

24 She admitted her homework was very late. ________

25 The apple tree was in the back garden. ________

5

Find and underline the two words which need to change places for the sentence to make sense.

B 17

**Example** She went to letter the write.

26 The leg of the broken was chair.

27 Have enough got you?

28 Untidy writing is very my.

29 What now you want do?

30 Cup make another I'll of tea.

5

Give the missing numbers in the following sequences.

B 23

| | | | | | | |
|---|---|---|---|---|---|---|
| **Example** | 2 | 4 | 6 | 8 | 10 | 12 |
| 31 | ___ | 59 | 67 | 75 | ___ | 91 |
| 32 | 105 | ___ | ___ | 45 | 25 | 5 |
| 33 | ___ | 96 | 84 | 72 | ___ | 48 |
| 34 | 46 | 42 | 38 | ___ | 30 | ___ |
| 35 | 15 | 20 | 21 | 26 | ___ | ___ |

5

Fill in the crosswords so that all the given words are included. You have been given one letter as a clue in each crossword.

B 19

36

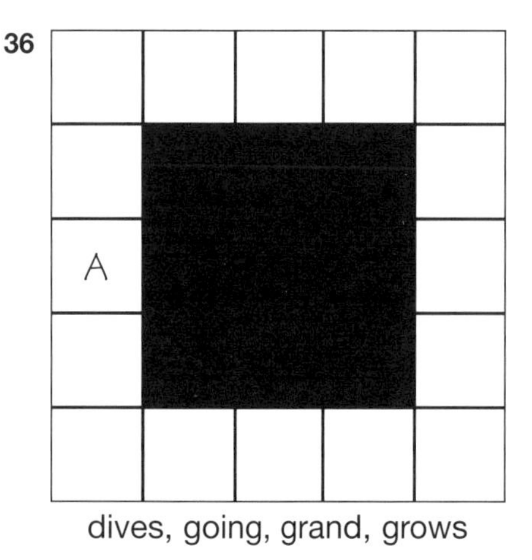


dives, going, grand, grows

37

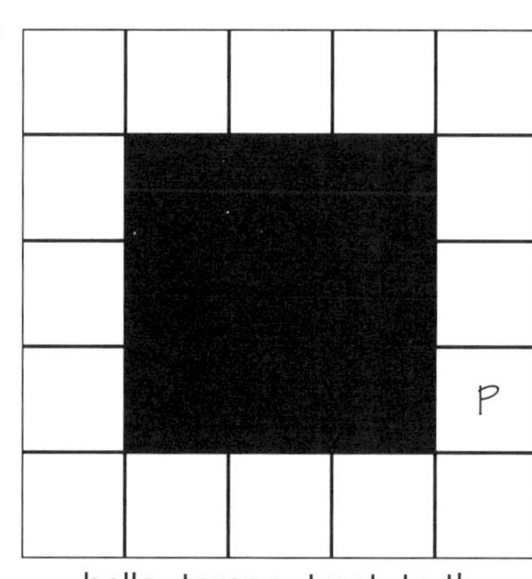


hello, tempo, treat, truth

**38**

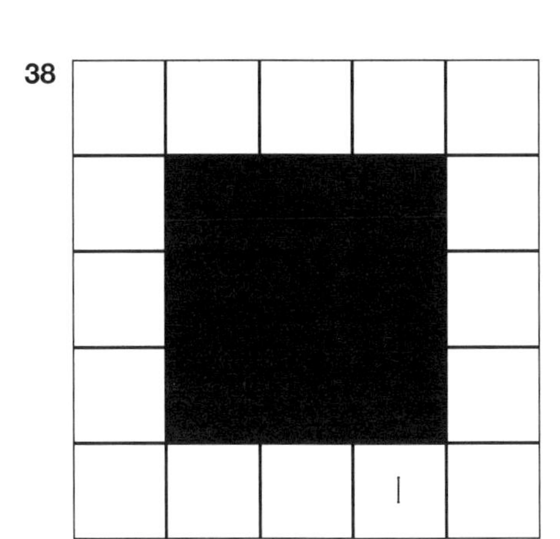


digit, first, fried, trust

**39**

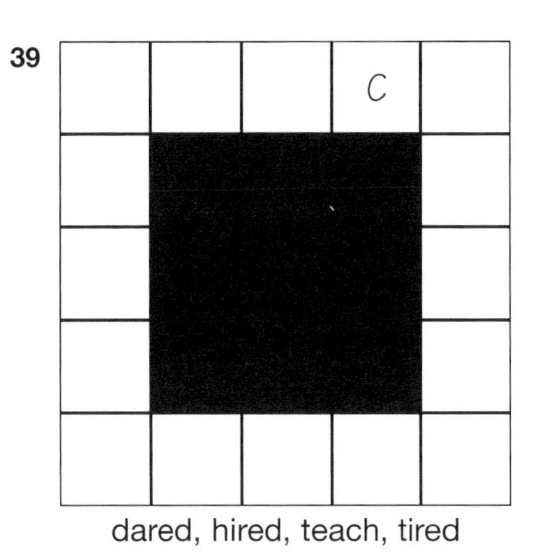


dared, hired, teach, tired

**40**

lifts, notes, quiet, thief

5

Choose two words, one from each set of brackets, to complete the sentences in the best way.

B 15

**Example** Tall is to (tree, <u>short</u>, colour) as narrow is to (thin, white, <u>wide</u>).

**41** Tiny is to (large, minute, second) as broad is to (wide, fast, country).

**42** Kind is to (unkind, generous, thoughtful) as slow is to (drive, quiet, quick).

**43** Clean is to (cloth, spot, dirty) as bottom is to (top, lowest, chest).

**44** Foot is to (hand, toe, knee) as hand is to (nail, leg, finger).

**45** Cat is to (catfood, paws, whiskers) as fish is to (water, fins, net).

5

If the code for T E A C H is + − × ÷ @, what are the codes for the following words?

B 24

**46** CAT ______________ **47** HAT ______________

What do these codes stand for?

**48** + − × ______________ **49** − × + ______________ **50** ÷ @ − × + ______________

5

Choose the word or phrase that makes each sentence true.

**Example** A LIBRARY always has (posters, a carpet, books, DVDs, stairs).

**51** A SANDWICH always has (ham, lettuce, bread, tomato, butter).

**52** A HORSE always has (hoofs, hay, a rider, a saddle, a stable).

**53** A CAR always has (air conditioning, a radio, a CD player, four doors, wheels).

**54** A BEACH always has (sand, umbrellas, chairs, plants, water).

**55** A BOOK always has (drawings, pages, photographs, stories, poems).

Underline two words, one from each group, that go together to form a new word. The word in the first group always comes first.

| | | |
|---|---|---|
| **Example** | (hand, green, for) | (light, house, sure) |
| **56** | (along, side, down) | (shot, stairs, wall) |
| **57** | (long, month, week) | (time, off, end) |
| **58** | (torch, gold, hot) | (burn, streak, light) |
| **59** | (must, left, pass) | (age, only, know) |
| **60** | (he, self, man) | (mind, or, and) |
| **61** | (girl, life, run) | (high, watch, guard) |
| **62** | (set, lift, kit) | (ten, hand, glow) |

Rearrange the muddled letters in capitals to make a proper word. The answer will complete the sentence sensibly.

**Example** A BEZAR is an animal with stripes. ZEBRA

**63** Please don't walk on the AGRSS. ________

**64** My favourite flower is the SORE. ________

**65** Be careful when you cut with a EIKFN. ________

***Now go to the Progress Chart to record your score!*** **Total** ___ **65**

# Paper 4

Underline the two words, one from each group, which are closest in meaning.

| | | |
|---|---|---|
| **Example** | (race, shop, start) | (finish, begin, end) |
| **1** | (health, remedy, doctor) | (chemist, right, cure) |
| **2** | (disturb, drill, hasty) | (slow, upset, rush) |
| **3** | (tell, offer, demand) | (insist, charge, buy) |
| **4** | (travel, area, map) | (direction, house, region) |
| **5** | (vast, heavy, size) | (huge, shape, inches) |

Find the three-letter word which can be added to the letters in capitals to make a new word. The new word will complete the sentence sensibly.

B 22

**Example** The cat sprang onto the MO. USE

**6** Callum is in HOSAL as he broke his arm. ________

**7–8** Ethan enjoys eating lots of GES and OGES. ________ ________

**9–10** Clare would RAT have some EAPPLE. ________ ________

5

Find the letter which will end the first word and start the second word.

B 10

**Example** peac ( h ) ome

**11** luc ( __ ) now

**12** las ( __ ) ive

**13** lam ( __ ) rince

**14** han ( __ ) ice

**15** fin ( __ ) ee

5

Here are five words. They can have a prefix of either SOME or BACK. Write S or B.

B 11

**16** __ ground

**17** __ body

**18** __ fire

**19** __ hand

**20** __ how

5

Write the four-letter word hidden at the end of one word and the beginning of the next word. The order of the letters may not be changed.

B 21

**Example** The children had bats and balls. sand

**21** All airports must be warned. ________

**22** I was sure he had one. ________

**23** They are stored in the shed. ________

**24** The rest of them went home. ________

**25** If you don't want a pear change it for an apple. ________

5

Change the first word of the third pair in the same way as the other pairs to give a new word.

B 18

**Example** bind, hind bare, hare but, hut

**26** pack, peck ball, bell band, ________

**27** sing, wing sink, wink sail, ________

**28** mile, lime sent, nest love, ________

**29** peal, pale bear, bare deal, ________

**30** hate, heat fowl, flow hire, ________

5

Complete the following sentences by selecting the most sensible word from each group of words given in the brackets. Underline the words selected.

**Example** The (children, books, foxes) carried the (houses, books, steps) home from the (greengrocer, library, factory).

**31** The boy (grows, talks, likes) to eat (tomato sauce, ice cream, biscuits) with his (fork, plate, pasta).

**32** The workman (knocked, pasted, glued) a large (hole, board, table) in the (wall, window, carpet) of his house.

**33** The (river, road, moat) flowed (above, under, round) the (sky, bird, bridge).

**34** John (tried, caught, dropped) to catch the (rope, ball, dog) before it (scored, lost, bounced).

**35** The (giant, dwarf, queen) was so (clever, tall, ugly) he could touch the (ground, clouds, frog).

Find and underline the two words which need to change places for the sentence to make sense.

**Example** She went to letter the write.

**36** Up try to clean it do.

**37** Her writing a letter to I'm.

**38** I like me book you gave the.

**39** The better is weather now.

**40** Acting you like do?

Find the missing number by using the two numbers outside the brackets in the same way as the other sets of numbers.

| | | | |
|---|---|---|---|
| **Example** | 2 [8] 4 | 3 [18] 6 | 5 [25] 5 |
| **41** | 18 [3] 6 | 20 [5] 4 | 16 [___] 8 |
| **42** | 2 [18] 9 | 3 [12] 4 | 6 [___] 4 |
| **43** | 11 [14] 3 | 5 [5] 0 | 8 [___] 7 |
| **44** | 10 [100] 10 | 4 [16] 4 | 8 [___] 8 |
| **45** | 13 [2] 11 | 10 [6] 4 | 9 [___] 8 |

Give the two missing groups of letters and numbers in the following sequences. The alphabet has been written out to help you.

A B C D E F G H I J K L M N O P Q R S T U V W X Y Z

| | | | | | | |
|---|---|---|---|---|---|---|
| **Example** | CQ | DP | EQ | FP | GQ | HP |
| **46** | A2 | C4 | ___ | ___ | I10 | K12 |
| **47** | Az | ___ | Cx | Dw | ___ | Fu |
| **48** | GA | HB | ___ | ___ | KE | LF |
| **49** | Za | Yb | Xa | ___ | ___ | Ub |
| **50** | ___ | E15 | I12 | M9 | Q6 | ___ |

5

Here are the number codes for four words. Match the right word to the right code.

R I N K    K I N    I N K    R A N K

935    7159    7359    359

**51** R I N K ________    **52** R A N K ________

**53** I N K ________    **54** K I N ________

**55** Using the same code, which of these stands for NEAR?

3617    5717    5617    ________

B 24

5

Rearrange the letters of the word in capitals to make another word. The new word has something to do with the first two words.

| | | | | |
|---|---|---|---|---|
| **Example** | spot | soil | SAINT | STAIN |
| **56** | running | contest | CARE | ________ |
| **57** | hazard | risk | GARDEN | ________ |
| **58** | story | fable | LATE | ________ |
| **59** | selfish | nasty | NAME | ________ |
| **60** | weary | exhausted | TRIED | ________ |

B 16

5

If a = 10, b = 6, c = 3 and d = 2, find the answer to the following calculations.

**61** $a - d =$ ___

**62** $a \times c =$ ___

**63** $a \div d =$ ___

**64** $a + b + c =$ ___

**65** $\frac{b}{c} =$ ___

B 26

5

***Now go to the Progress Chart to record your score!*** **Total** 65

# Paper 5

**1–5** Look at these groups.

| M | G | C |
|---|---|---|
| Money | Gardening tools | Carpentry tools |

Choose the correct group for each of the words below. Write the letter.

| | | | | | | | |
|---|---|---|---|---|---|---|---|
| barrow | ___ | pound | ___ | dime | ___ | chisel | ___ |
| hammer | ___ | fork | ___ | spade | ___ | dollar | ___ |
| trowel | ___ | cent | ___ | | | | |

B 1

5

Find the three-letter word which can be added to the letters in capitals to make a new word. The new word will complete the sentence sensibly.

**Example** The cat sprang onto the MO. USE

6 That's a big parcel. It says on it 'HLE with care'. ________

7 The DINGS on the walls were beautiful. ________

8 The trees in the FST were really huge. ________

9 She PRISED piano every day. ________

10 I am SED of monsters. ________

B 22

5

Find the letter which will end the first word and start the second word.

**Example** peac ( h ) ome

11 pian ( __ ) pen 12 mean ( __ ) here

13 heal ( __ ) eat 14 fas ( __ ) ick 15 spor ( __ ) idy

B 10

5

If these words were written backwards and then placed in alphabetical order, which word would come fifth? Underline your answer.

| | | | | | |
|---|---|---|---|---|---|
| 16 | slowly | happily | softly | friendly | normally |
| 17 | glanced | misplaced | polished | showed | charged |
| 18 | blacksmith | fifth | health | truth | warmth |
| 19 | vitamin | javelin | entertain | satin | captain |
| 20 | parent | absent | accident | confront | vacant |

B 20

5

Write the four-letter word hidden at the end of one word and the beginning of the next word. The order of the letters may not be changed.

**Example** The children had bats and balls. sand

21 I heard a crash in your bedroom. ________

22 I started it at once. ________

23 My son likes to write stories. ________

24 When one dog barks the others all join in. ________

25 We started to dance as soon as music played. ________

B 21

5

Add one letter to the word in capital letters to make a new word. The meaning of the new word is given in the clue.

**Example** PLAN simple plain

26 TOOL three-legged seat ________

27 FIEND a person one likes ________

28 CLAP to hold together firmly ________

29 CAST along the seashore ________

30 SAY to remain ________

B 12

5

Complete the following sentences by selecting the most sensible word from each group of words given in the brackets. Underline the words selected.

B 14

**Example** The (children, books, foxes) carried the (houses, books, steps) home from the (greengrocer, library, factory).

**31** The old man likes to eat (potatoes, rice pudding, bananas) before he goes to (work, garden, sleep) but he can't find a place to leave the (cores, peel, skins) near his bed.

**32** This (afternoon, yesterday, house) we are going on a school (desk, visit, yard) to the town (museum, railings, sky).

**33** Can't you be (good, quick, quiet)? You're too (big, clumsy, noisy). I'm trying to (cook, play, work).

**34** When on holiday I like to (visit, buy, sell) souvenirs so that I when I get (home, away, tired) I (forget, remember, enjoy) what a good time I had.

**35** The (fire brigade, police, vet) came quickly to the (farm, animals, blaze) with their (dogs, hats, hoses).

5

Choose two words, one from each set of brackets, to complete the sentence in the best way.

B 15

**Example** Tall is to (tree, short, colour) as narrow is to (thin, white, wide).

**36** Same is to (similar, opposite, change) as day is to (long, night, sleep).

**37** Add is to (number, subtract, plus) as divide is to (share, multiply, figures).

**38** Expand is to (lessen, shrink, widen) as reduce is to (cover, unfold, shorten).

**39** Unite is to (slit, repair, join) as new is to (modern, old, out of date).

**40** Finish is to (rest, end, lose) as magnificent is to (damaged, grand, terrible).

5

Underline the two words, one from each group, which are closest in meaning.

B 5

| | | |
|---|---|---|
| **Example** | (race, shop, start) | (finish, begin, end) |
| **41** | (hotel, prison, house) | (office, jail, roof) |
| **42** | (difficult, short, slow) | (long, hard, never) |
| **43** | (present, empty, maybe) | (here, full, absent) |
| **44** | (big, heavy, remote) | (tiny, flat, distant) |
| **45** | (halt, recent, permanent) | (distant, temporary, stop) |

5

If the code for S T E A M is a b c d e, what are the codes for the following words?

B 24

**46** M A S T ____________ **47** T A M E ____________

What do these codes stand for?

**48** e c a a ____________ **49** e d b c ____________ **50** a c d b ____________

5

If $a = 2$, $b = 3$, $d = 4$, $e = 5$, $f = 6$, $g = 8$, find the value of these words.

Give your answers as letters.

**51** $g - b =$ ___ **52** $f \div a =$ ___ **53** $(e + d) - f =$ ___

**54** $2a =$ ___ **55** $a + b =$ ___

Underline the one word in the brackets which will go equally well with both the pairs of words outside the brackets.

| | | | |
|---|---|---|---|
| **Example** | rush, attack | cost, fee | (price, hasten, strike, <u>charge</u>, money) |
| **56** | apartment, rooms | level, even | (flat, home, smooth, habitat, ledge) |
| **57** | clue, lead | central, important | (hint, lock, key, trail, essential) |
| **58** | apple, grape | red, yellow | (pear, pineapple, brown, rose, orange) |
| **59** | price, debt | beak, snout | (invoice, leaflet, nose, paw, bill) |
| **60** | stone, boulder | sway, move | (cliff, hill, swing, step, rock) |

Change one word so that the sentence makes sense. Underline the word you are taking out and write your new word on the line.

**Example** I waited in line to buy a <u>book</u> to see the film. *ticket*

**61** She put the milk in the oven to keep it cool. ________

**62** My dog laughs when people ring the doorbell. ________

**63** I put a coin on the envelope before I posted it. ________

**64** The bicycle's saddles went round and round. ________

**65** November is the last month of the year. ________

***Now go to the Progress Chart to record your score!*** **Total** 65

# Paper 6

Underline the two words which are the odd ones out in the following groups of words.

| | | | | | |
|---|---|---|---|---|---|
| **Example** | black | <u>king</u> | purple | green | <u>house</u> |
| **1** | house | road | bungalow | castle | path |
| **2** | swim | coat | sweater | dive | t-shirt |
| **3** | kneel | sit | walk | hop | skip |
| **4** | butter | cake | bread | bun | flour |
| **5** | onion | apple | plum | cabbage | potato |

Find the three-letter word which can be added to the letters in capitals to make a new word. The new word will complete the sentence sensibly.

B 22

**Example** The cat sprang onto the MO. USE

6 I cycled along a NAR lane. ________

7 I'm thirsty, time to stop for a DR. ________

8 She wouldn't listen. I T her she'd have to do it. ________

9 We saw a polar B at the zoo. ________

10 H grows on our heads. ________

5

Find the letter which will end the first word and start the second word.

B 10

**Example** peac ( h ) ome

11 spen ( __ ) anger

12 mos ( __ ) ribe

13 lea ( __ ) lood

14 stra ( __ ) ood

15 firs ( __ ) ender

5

Underline the one word which **cannot be made** from the letters of the word in capital letters.

B 7

| | | | | | | |
|---|---|---|---|---|---|---|
| **Example** | STATIONERY | stone | tyres | ration | nation | noisy |
| 16 | TERRACE | car | rate | trace | erase | crate |
| 17 | DISTANT | stead | stand | stain | ants | dint |
| 18 | PAINTER | trip | rain | tramp | nape | print |
| 19 | GENERAL | large | near | rage | gear | ages |
| 20 | DETAINS | staid | instead | near | neat | site |

5

Write the four-letter word hidden at the end of one word and the beginning of the next word. The order of the letters may not be changed.

B 21

**Example** The children had bats and balls. sand

21 Harry's top was covered in mud. ________

22 We are not going there. ________

23 The shops will be open so we will go tomorrow. ________

24 Stars and angels gave the sign. ________

25 As it is raining shall we eat lunch inside? ________

5

Change the first word of the third pair in the same way as the other pairs to give a new word.

B 18

**Example** bind, hind bare, hare but, hut

26 tint, stint trap, strap tale, ________

| | | |
|---|---|---|
| **27** gate, grate | pick, prick | tick, ________ |
| **28** same, lame | sate, late | sack, ________ |
| **29** same, mate | bare, rate | page, ________ |
| **30** grip, rip | blot, lot | ship, ________ |

Find and underline the two words which need to change places for the sentence to make sense.

**Example** She went to letter the write.

**31** I am this up with fed food.

**32** Were chess playing they?

**33** Did win team the or lose?

**34** Let's my to go house.

**35** Where it I put shall?

Choose two words, one from each set of brackets, to complete the sentence in the best way.

**Example** Smile is to happiness as (drink, tear, shout) is to (whisper, laugh, sorrow).

**36** Today is to yesterday as (May, June, July) is to (August, May, March).

**37** Two is to hands as (4, 5, 10) is to (toes, ears, thumbs).

**38** Roof is to house as (window, wall, ceiling) is to (cover, room, floor).

**39** Black is to white as (snow, rain, cold) is to (hot, sun, warm).

**40** Cat is to animal as (dog, robin, cow) is to (air, bird, fish).

Fill in the crosswords so that all the given words are included. You have been given one letter as a clue in each crossword.

**41**

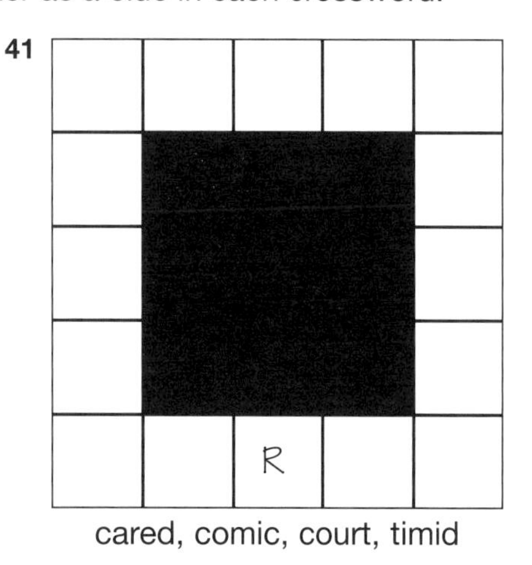


cared, comic, court, timid

**42**

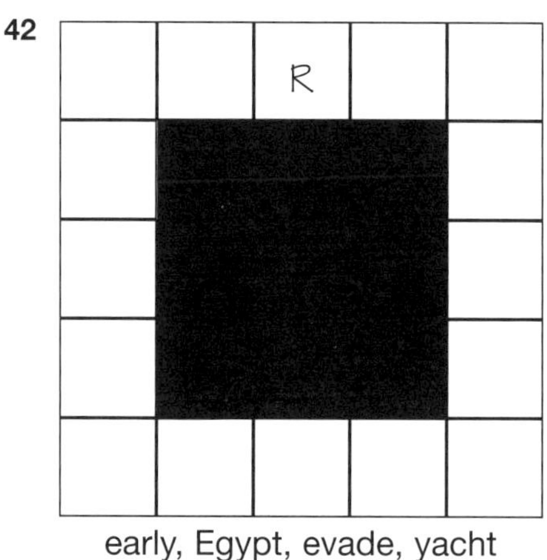


early, Egypt, evade, yacht

43

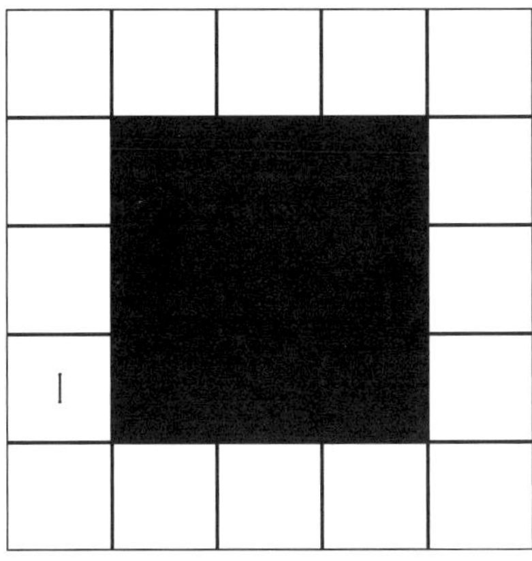


clear, madam, major, music

44

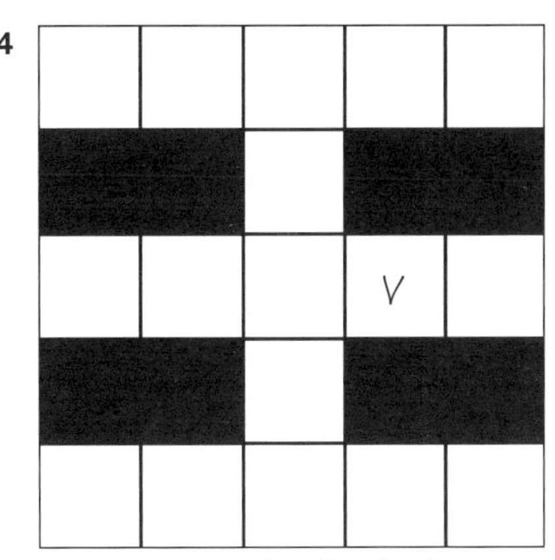


prove, pushy, treat, store

45

meals, motor, repay, plant

5

B 20

If the letters in the following words were arranged in alphabetical order, which letter would come in the middle?

**46** gruel ____________

**47** exhaust ____________

If these words were listed in reverse alphabetical order, which word would come second?

| | | | | |
|---|---|---|---|---|
| **48** charade | chorus | chamber | chemist | chivalry |
| **49** fraction | friction | frostbite | frown | friend |
| **50** trampoline | train | trophy | treasure | trellis |

5

If a = 1, b = 2, c = 3, d = 4, e = 5, f = 6, find the value of the following calculations.

**51** abc = ___

**52** cde = ___

**53** bcd = ___

**54** ef = ___

**55** cf + be = ___

5

Solve the problems by working out the letter codes. The alphabet has been written out to help you.

B 24

A B C D E F G H I J K L M N O P Q R S T U V W X Y Z

**Example** In a code, SECOND is written as UGEQPF. How would you write THIRD? VJKTF

56 In a code, ARRIVE is written as ZQQHUD. How would you write REAR? ________

57 In a code, LISTEN is written as MJTUFO. How would you write NEST? ________

58 In a code, PLANE is written as RNCPG. What does NCR mean? ________

59 In a code, BEAR is written as ADZQ. How would you write KING? ________

60 In a code, VOWEL is written as UNVDK. What does EHMC mean? ________

5

Which one letter can be added to the front of all of these words to make new words?

B 12

**Example** care cat crate call

| | | | | |
|---|---|---|---|---|
| 61 | __eat | __one | __ice | __ote |
| 62 | __ail | __ape | __ear | __here |
| 63 | __act | __lag | __all | __ace |
| 64 | __ill | __end | __lack | __last |
| 65 | __air | __all | __and | __old |

5

***Now go to the Progress Chart to record your score!*** **Total** 65

# Paper 7

Underline the word in the brackets closest in meaning to the word in capitals.

B 5

**Example** UNHAPPY (unkind death laughter sad friendly)

1 EDGE (centre outside rim bottom top)

2 DOZE (blanket start nap bed awake)

3 LITTER (bins sweep brush rubbish paper)

4 DIFFICULT (easy understand answer soft hard)

5 TALE (book story read paper library)

5

Underline the pair of words most opposite in meaning.

B 9

**Example** cup, mug coffee, milk hot, cold

6 tall, high wide, narrow long, thin

7 hot, warm clean, tidy near, far

| | | | |
|---|---|---|---|
| **8** | deep, shallow | rush, hurry | occupy, fill |
| **9** | open, shut | pause, stop | provide, supply |
| **10** | leave, exit | borrow, lend | damp, moist |

5

Find the letter which will end the first word and start the second word.

B 10

**Example** peac ( h ) ome

**11** gon ( __ ) low  **12** hav ( __ ) ver  **13** pas ( __ ) ave

**14** man ( __ ) ard  **15** los ( __ ) ray

5

Find a word that can be put in front of each of the following words to make new, compound words.

B 11

| | | | | | |
|---|---|---|---|---|---|
| **Example** | cast | fall | ward | pour | down |
| **16** | show | board | light | step | ______ |
| **17** | look | line | back | board | ______ |
| **18** | sleep | take | rule | priced | ______ |
| **19** | noon | care | taste | thought | ______ |
| **20** | bike | car | way | boat | ______ |

5

Write the four-letter word hidden at the end of one word and the beginning of the next word. The order of the letters may not be changed.

B 21

**Example** The children had bats and balls. sand

**21** Some of his ideas were quite wrong. ______

**22** My temperature was back to normal this morning. ______

**23** First of all we will wash up. ______

**24** I wish other people would pick up their rubbish. ______

**25** There was a large wasp in the jam. ______

5

Change the first word into the last word by changing one letter at a time and making a new, different word in the middle.

B 13

| | | | |
|---|---|---|---|
| **Example** | CASE | CASH | LASH |
| **26** | FISH | ______ | FAST |
| **27** | LOAN | ______ | TOAD |
| **28** | CODE | ______ | HOPE |
| **29** | FILL | ______ | MILK |
| **30** | WILD | ______ | SILT |

5

Complete the following sentences by selecting the most sensible word from each group of words given in the brackets. Underline the words selected.

B 14

**Example** The (children, books, foxes) carried the (houses, books, steps) home from the (greengrocer, library, factory).

**31** Every (day, morning, birthday) my (dog, cat, mother) makes me a special (loaf, cake, bun).

**32** The woman (sighed, screamed, sang) as she was so (hot, cold, frightened) by the scary (rug, film, mug)

**33** The secret (door, stairway, message) had been written on the (hand, cupboard, parchment) by the (mother, mouse, pirate).

**34** He (wrote, thought, ran) as quickly as possible to the (cows, stones, police) to raise the (price, roof, alarm).

**35** 'Put your (feet, sticks, hands) up if you know the (question, time, answer),' said the (king, friend, teacher).

5

Find and underline the two words which need to change places for each sentence to make sense.

B 17

**Example** She went to letter the write.

**36** My beautifully is work neat.

**37** The badly is carpet stained.

**38** Can you turn volume the down?

**39** Some was given I flowers.

**40** Don't to try move please.

5

Solve the problems by working out the letter codes. The alphabet has been written out to help you.

B 24

A B C D E F G H I J K L M N O P Q R S T U V W X Y Z

**Example** In a code, SECOND is written as UGEQPF. How would you write THIRD? VJKTF

**41** In a code, CHILDREN is written as DIJMESFO. How would you write RIDE? ______

**42** In a code, PLEASE is written as RNGCUG. How would you write LEAP? ______

**43** In a code, STEP is written as TUFQ. How would you write COAL? ______

**44** In a code, DUST is written as BSQR. What does BMMP mean? ______

**45** In a code, MILK is written as OKNM. What does VKR mean? ______

5

Fill in the crosswords so that all the given words are included. You have been given one letter as a clue in each crossword.

B 19

**46**

| | | | | |
|---|---|---|---|---|
| ■ | ■ | | ■ | ■ |
| | | | | |
| ■ | ■ | | ■ | ■ |
| | | T | | |

house, laser, litre, upset

**47**

| | | | T | |
|---|---|---|---|---|
| ■ | ■ | | ■ | ■ |
| | | | | |
| ■ | ■ | | ■ | ■ |
| | | | | |

greed, lapse, paste, steep

**48**

| | | | | |
|---|---|---|---|---|
| ■ | ■ | | ■ | ■ |
| | | | | |
| ■ | ■ | E | ■ | ■ |
| | | | | |

fudge, march, order, stone

**49**

| | | | | |
|---|---|---|---|---|
| ■ | ■ | | ■ | ■ |
| | | | | |
| ■ | ■ | | ■ | ■ |
| | L | | | |

allow, expel, super, trees

**50**

| | | | A | |
|---|---|---|---|---|
| ■ | ■ | | ■ | ■ |
| | | | | |
| ■ | ■ | | ■ | ■ |
| | | | | |

bread, catch, enter, farms

5

If these words were listed in reverse alphabetical order, which word would come second?

B 20

**51** clasp clamp close cloak clock ________

**52** empty glass fruit glove elect ________

If these words were placed in alphabetical order, which word would come fourth?

| | | | | | |
|---|---|---|---|---|---|
| **53** human | hound | honey | house | hours | ________ |
| **54** region | parade | patrol | reason | reader | ________ |

4

If e = 1, f = 2, d = 3, c = 4, b = 6, a = 9, find the answer to the following calculations.

B 26

**55** $c - d =$ ___ **56** $b + e =$ ___ **57** $2a - e =$ ___

**58** $\frac{b}{f} =$ ___ **59** $ad =$ ___ **60** $bc - a =$ ___

6

Which of the following form words when spelt backwards? Underline them.

B 20

| | | | | |
|---|---|---|---|---|
| **61** MUST | MOOR | MALE | MIST | MARK |
| **62** WINK | WENT | WANT | WAKE | WOLF |
| **63** TRAP | MEWS | MILL | MONK | MAST |
| **64** PADS | PENS | PEAS | SEED | SWAP |
| **65** EMIT | TUNE | AMID | EXIT | TINT |

5

***Now go to the Progress Chart to record your score!*** **Total** 65

# Paper 8

Look at these three groups.

B 1

| A | B | C |
|---|---|---|
| Flowers | Fruit | Trees |

**1–5** Choose the correct group for each of the words below. Write in the letter.

| | | | |
|---|---|---|---|
| grape ___ | ash ___ | bluebell ___ | elm ___ |
| lily ___ | melon ___ | willow ___ | kiwi ___ |
| oak ___ | crocus ___ | | |

5

Underline the pair of words most opposite in meaning.

B 9

**Example** cup, mug coffee, milk <u>hot, cold</u>

| | | |
|---|---|---|
| **6** east, west | disease, sickness | upset, worry |
| **7** sand, beach | black, white | street, road |
| **8** choose, select | omen, sign | divide, multiply |
| **9** whole, total | cheap, expensive | force, compel |
| **10** level, even | last, end | fail, succeed |

5

Find the letter which will end the first word and start the second word.

**Example** peac ( h ) ome

11 car ( ___ ) win  12 cal ( ___ ) ose  13 mes ( ___ ) hut

14 bea ( ___ ) rum  15 sho ( ___ ) ind

B 10

5

Underline two words, one from each group, that go together to form a new word. The word in the first group always comes first.

**Example** (hand, green, for) (light, house, sure)

16 (foot, grown, dear) (move, come, print)

17 (whole, quarter, half) (path, way, tumble)

18 (in, out, but) (break, crash, tumble)

19 (ear, eye, lid) (sign, scar, ache)

20 (wide, lag, broad) (chair, cast, road)

B 8

5

Write the four-letter word hidden at the end of one word and the beginning of the next word. The order of the letters may not be changed.

**Example** The children had bats and balls. sand

21 Ice helps lower the temperature of your drink. ________

22 Quickly come to the window and see the fireworks! ________

23 My homework is as easy to do as ever. ________

24 He asked me to move nearer. ________

25 Because the bus was so late, you're in a rush. ________

B 21

5

Change the first word into the last word by changing one letter at a time and making a new, different word in the middle.

**Example** CASE CASH LASH

26 RAIN ________ HAIL  27 SOME ________ COMB

28 THIN ________ THAT  29 WILL ________ FULL

30 PINE ________ FIND

B 13

5

Fill in the missing letters and numbers. The alphabet has been written out to help you.

A B C D E F G H I J K L M N O P Q R S T U V W X Y Z

**Example** AB is to CD as PQ is to RS.

31 AC is to BD as JL is to ________.

32 ACE is to CEG as LNP is to ________.

33 EH is to IL as MP is to ________.

34 5QR is to 6ST as 7UV is to ________.

35 3CE is to 5DF as 7EG is to ________.

B 23

5

Fill in the crosswords so that all the given words are included. You have been given one letter as a clue in each crossword.

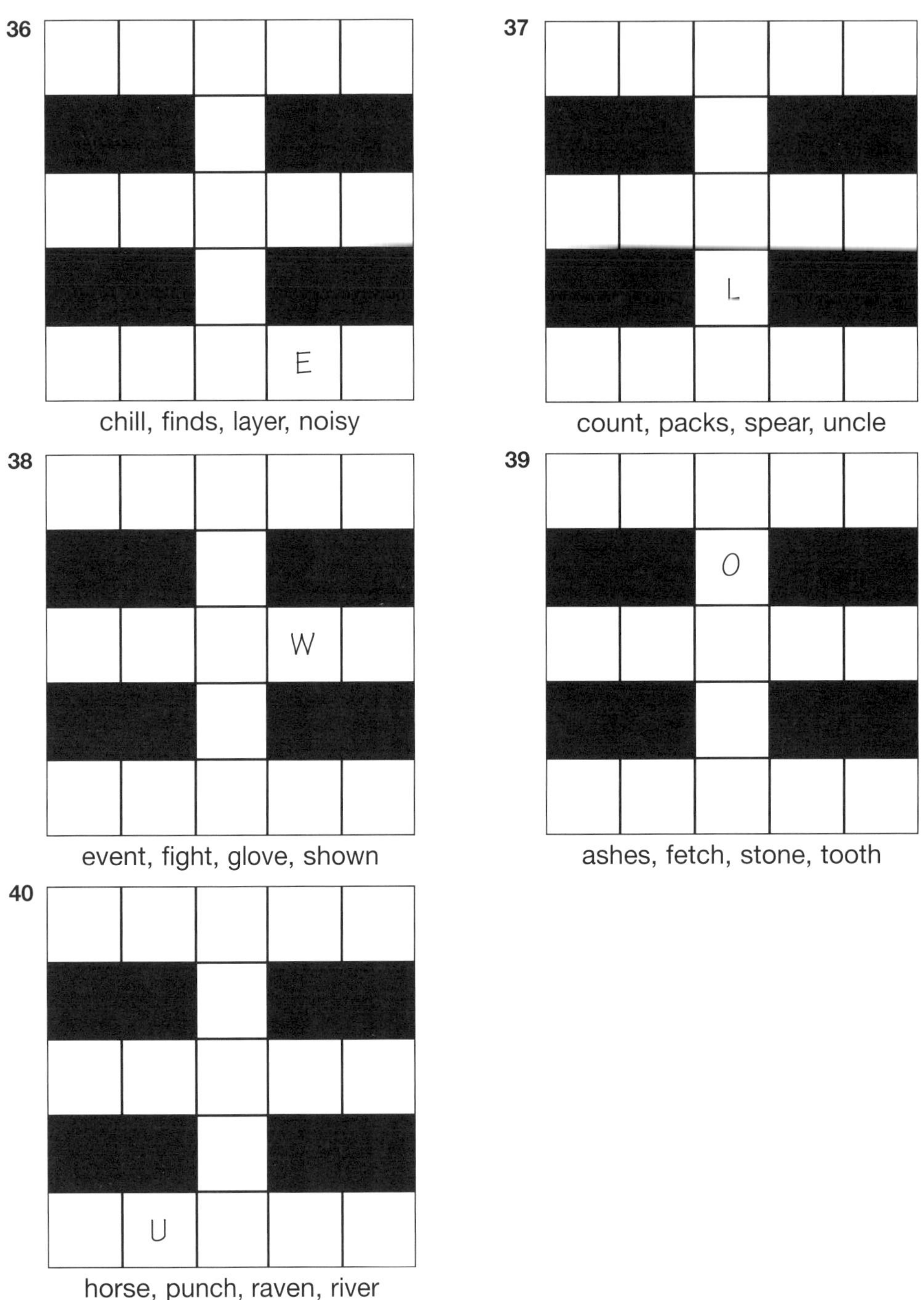


5

Underline the one word in brackets which will go equally well with both the pairs of words outside the brackets.

B 5

**Example** rush, attack cost, fee (price, hasten, strike, charge, money)

**41** protect, shield pillow, pad (sofa, bedding, cushion, bandage)

**42** smoulder, blaze shoot, detonate (trigger, excite, fire, launch)

## Paper 1

1 easy, simple
2 go, depart
3 new, fresh
4 tired, weary
5 hide, conceal
6 sell, purchase
7 dim, bright
8 back, front
9 question, answer
10 accept, refuse
11 farmer, shed, milk the cows
12 spade, beach, castle
13 forget, post, letter
14 eagle, food, nest
15 lantern, face, buried
16 PLATE, PETAL
17 SHORE, HORSE
18 TABLE, BLEAT
19 HEADS, SHADE
20 LEAST, STALE
21 ever
22 hero
23 rear
24 soft
25 ends
26 e
27 k
28 t
29 l
30 t
31 today, feel
32 tights, it
33 hairdo, your
34 glass, I've
35 home, have
36 GH
37 JL
38 P8
39 18BC
40 2DE
41 f
42 s
43 w
44 p
45 d

46–50

POLES
PLUMP
STAND
POUND

51 * : ! ?
52 £ : ! *
53 / ! : £
54 TRAP
55 REAL
56 beak
57 roots
58 sole
59 walls
60 sleeves
61 tree
62 lean
63 sand
64 fame
65 spin

## Paper 2

1 alter, change
2 fear, fright
3 fidget, wriggle
4 hard, difficult
5 start, begin
6 shiny, dull
7 generous, mean
8 home, away
9 often, seldom
10 raise, lower
11 nameless
12 keepsake
13 behead
14 textbook
15 keyboard
16 TEA
17 ROW
18 EAT
19 ARM
20 ASK
21 scan
22 heal
23 herb
24 item
25 them
26 SAND
27 MAKE
28 DEAL
29 BALL
30 COME
31 sheep, field, grass
32 tiger, cage, zoo
33 stone, frog, flies
34 old, up, steep
35 move, snake, rock
36 April, May
37 lamb, sheep
38 artist, picture
39 cup, drink
40 uncle, nephew

41–45

46 82, 55
47 $\frac{1}{2}$, 1
48 63, 56
49 99,110
50 7, 8
51 ○△❞
52 △❞◆
53 ○■❞
54 △❞
55 ○■❞◆
56 b
57 l
58 e
59 t
60 g
61 ACHE
62 BEGIN
63 BELOW
64 CHEAP
65 MALE

## Paper 3

1 hail
2 stable
3 carrots
4 speak
5 toddlers
6 spend, save
7 same, different
8 quit, start
9 crowded, deserted
10 hurt, heal
11 e
12 t
13 d
14 r
15 l
16 foot
17 up
18 book
19 in
20 head
21 tool
22 mesh
23 them
24 head
25 heap
26 broken, chair
27 enough, you
28 untidy, my
29 now, do
30 cup, I'll
31 51 83
32 85 65
33 108 60
34 34 26
35 27 32
36–40

41 minute, wide
42 unkind, quick
43 dirty, top
44 toe, finger
45 paws, fins
46 ÷ × +
47 @ × +
48 TEA
49 EAT
50 CHEAT
51 bread
52 hoofs
53 wheels
54 water
55 pages
56 downstairs
57 weekend
58 torchlight
59 passage
60 manor
61 lifeguard
62 kitten
63 GRASS
64 ROSE
65 KNIFE

## Paper 4

1 remedy, cure
2 disturb, upset
3 demand, insist
4 area, region
5 vast, huge
6 PIT
7 RAP
8 RAN
9 HER
10 PIN
11 k
12 h
13 p
14 d
15 s
16 B
17 S
18 B
19 B
20 S
21 lair
22 done
23 rest
24 here
25 arch
26 bend
27 wail
28 vole
29 dale
30 heir
31 likes, tomato sauce, pasta
32 knocked, hole, wall
33 river, under, bridge
34 tried, ball, bounced
35 giant, tall, clouds
36 up, do
37 her, I'm
38 me, the
39 better, weather
40 acting, do
41 2
42 24
43 15
44 64
45 1
46 E6 G8
47 By Ev
48 IC JD
49 Wb Va
50 A18 U3
51 7359
52 7159
53 359
54 935
55 5617
56 RACE
57 DANGER
58 TALE
59 MEAN
60 TIRED
61 8
62 30
63 5
64 19
65 2

## Paper 5

1–5 *Give one mark for each two correct answers:* barrow G, pound M, dime M, chisel C, hammer C, fork G, spade G, dollar M, trowel G, cent M
6 AND
7 RAW
8 ORE
9 ACT
10 CAR
11 o
12 t
13 s
14 t
15 t
16 slowly
17 showed
18 truth
19 satin
20 confront
21 shin
22 edit
23 test
24 none
25 west
26 stool
27 friend
28 clamp or clasp
29 coast
30 stay
31 bananas, sleep, skins
32 afternoon, visit, museum

33 quiet, noisy, work
34 buy, home, remember
35 fire brigade, blaze, hoses
36 opposite, night
37 subtract, multiply
38 widen, shorten
39 join, modern
40 end, grand
41 prison, jail
42 difficult, hard
43 present, here
44 remote, distant
45 halt, stop
46 edab
47 bdec
48 MESS
49 MATE
50 SEAT
51 e
52 b
53 b
54 d
55 e
56 flat
57 key
58 orange
59 bill
60 rock
61 oven, fridge
62 laughs, barks
63 coin, stamp
64 saddles, wheels
65 November, December

## Paper 6

1 road, path
2 swim, dive
3 kneel, sit
4 butter, flour
5 apple, plum
6 ROW
7 INK
8 OLD
9 EAR
10 AIR
11 d
12 t
13 f
14 w
15 t
16 erase
17 stead
18 tramp
19 ages
20 near
21 stop
22 wear
23 pens
24 sand
25 chin
26 stale
27 trick
28 lack
29 gate
30 hip
31 this, fed
32 chess, they
33 win, the
34 my, go
35 it, shall
36 June, May
37 10, toes
38 ceiling, room
39 cold, hot
40 robin, bird

41–45

46 l
47 s
48 chivalry
49 frostbite
50 trellis
51 6
52 60
53 24
54 30
55 28
56 QDZQ
57 OFTU
58 LAP
59 JHMF
60 FIND
61 n
62 t
63 f
64 b
65 h

## Paper 7

1 rim
2 nap
3 rubbish
4 hard
5 story
6 wide, narrow
7 near, far
8 deep, shallow
9 open, shut
10 borrow, lend
11 g
12 e
13 s
14 y
15 t
16 side
17 out
18 over
19 after
20 motor
21 side
22 malt
23 fall
24 shot
25 spin
26 FIST
27 LOAD
28 COPE
29 MILL
30 WILT
31 birthday, mother, cake
32 screamed, frightened, film
33 message, parchment, pirate
34 ran, police, alarm
35 hands, answer, teacher
36 beautifully, work
37 badly, carpet
38 volume, the
39 some, I
40 to, try
41 SJEF
42 NGCR
43 DPBM
44 DOOR
45 TIP

46–50

51 clock
52 glass
53 house
54 reason
55 1
56 7
57 17
58 3
59 27
60 15
61 MOOR
62 WOLF
63 TRAP
64 SWAP
65 EMIT

## Paper 8

1–5 *Give one mark for each two correct answers:* grape B, ash C, bluebell A, elm C, lily A, melon B, willow C, kiwi B, oak C, crocus A
6 east, west
7 black, white
8 divide, multiply
9 cheap, expensive
10 fail, succeed
11 t
12 l
13 s
14 d
15 w
16 footprint
17 halfway
18 outbreak
19 earache
20 broadcast
21 slow
22 wand
23 seas
24 oven
25 rein
26 RAIL
27 COME
28 THAN
29 FILL
30 FINE
31 KM
32 NPR
33 QT
34 8WX
35 9FH

36–40

41 cushion
42 fire
43 bright
44 net
45 spring
46 TIN
47 ORE
48 TWO
49 LOT
50 SAT
51 48
52 95
53 88
54 84
55 10
56 15
57 10
58 12
59 48
60 1
61 EINOQSTU
62 N
63 S
64 EIMPR
65 M

## Paper 9

1 power
2 coast
3 herd
4 collar
5 clock
6 BUTTER
7 GRUBBY
8 ELEPHANT
9 LITTER
10 ENVELOPES
11 AND
12 RIP
13 FUN
14 ARK
15 EAR
16 bat
17 cost
18 ever
19 pane
20 sing
21 oval
22 were
23 rope
24 itch
25 tone
26 ear, blink
27 pan, flit
28 and, flake
29 one, dwell
30 sun, petal
31 shirt, football, team
32 sharpener, bag, chair
33 ship, harbour, slowly
34 listened, hear, coming
35 Antarctic, huge, houses
36 29
37 14
38 1
39 24
40 72

41–45

46 STONE
47 DARE
48 SHRUB
49 CRATE
50 REAR
51 PIE
52 KIN
53 ARE
54 PAW
55 ACT
56 lonely

57 march
58 rascal
59 square
60 puppets
61–65 2 = Whites, 3 = Blues, 4 = Greys, 5 = Greens, 6 = Blacks

## Paper 10

1 bend, curve
2 small, slight
3 ruin, destroy
4 author, writer
5 fast, swift
6 BAG
7 ONE
8 APE
9 MAT
10 OAT
11 have
12 throb
13 core
14 rope
15 sand
16 hiss
17 mash
18 stir
19 meat
20 romp
21 far, cane
22 soil, peat
23 host, paint
24 hunt, laid
25 dear, sport
26 school, important, wonders
27 found, umbrella, rain
28 fire, building, quickly
29 cat, black, collar
30 drank, put on, left
31 better, weather
32 supper, looking
33 me, the
34 up, do
35 vase, knocked
36 D79
37 G20
38 F18
39 GH8
40 QRS
41 still, active
42 warm, cool
43 bend, straighten
44 fix, destroy
45 low, high
46 garland
47 gallop
48 g, a
49 gallop
50 6
51 l h j b
52 g h l b
53 DEAN
54 STAIN
55 guests
56 coat
57 food
58 a steering wheel
59 rules
60 add, reduce
61 lose, tie
62 catch, free
63 give, accept
64 command, request
65 delete, circle

## Paper 11

1 shout, yell
2 need, require
3 bench, chair
4 ask, enquire
5 close, shut
6 PEN
7 ASH
8 ARC
9 WAR
10 LIP
11 n
12 i
13 h
14 t
15 o
16 snow
17 hand
18 water
19 under
20 some
21 heap
22 iris
23 sold
24 none
25 wear
26 SLAY
27 CHAT
28 PAST
29 DIRE
30 LUCK
31 new, which
32 wet, towel
33 borrow, you
34 very, said
35 cover, like
36 numbers, letters
37 light, dark
38 run, fly
39 string, rope
40 flowers, vegetables

41–45

| U | N | F | I | T |
|---|---|---|---|---|
| N | ■ | I | ■ | ■ |
| T | R | E | A | T |
| I | ■ | L | ■ | ■ |
| L | A | D | E | N |

| P | ■ | F | ■ | S |
|---|---|---|---|---|
| A | L | L | O | W |
| R | ■ | A | ■ | E |
| K | ■ | K | ■ | L |
| S | P | E | L | L |

| L | A | D | L | E |
|---|---|---|---|---|
| ■ | ■ | R | ■ | V |
| T | R | I | B | E |
| ■ | ■ | V | ■ | N |
| G | R | E | A | T |

| R | O | B | E | S |
|---|---|---|---|---|
| ■ | ■ | E | ■ | P |
| C | R | A | T | E |
| ■ | ■ | C | ■ | A |
| O | T | H | E | R |

46 CN DO
47 5R 17Z
48 ZA WD
49 YR AN
50 GFE HGF
51 TEAR
52 PEST
53 MEAL
54 HOSE
55 BEARD
56 24
57 60
58 JMU
59 NUT
60 FUN
61 MDWS
62 IPMJEBZ
63 band
64 rough
65 sweet

## Paper 12

1 lead, iron
2 mountain, hill
3 cross, angry
4 sun, moon
5 rest, sleep
6 NOW
7 VAN
8 EAR
9 RIM
10 RAT
11 bluebell
12 sunshine
13 footstep
14 afterwards
15 football
16 pour
17 calf
18 chap
19 lint

20 etch
21 team, keys
22 flat, hero
23 tall, skin
24 bead, fore
25 pint, rate
26 tried, son, homework
27 sign, road, stop
28 plane, sky, flying
29 walked, fast, castle
30 highwaymen, coach, gold
31 NP
32 YZ
33 MOQ
34 DW
35 FGE
36–40

| W | H | I | T | E |
|---|---|---|---|---|
| A | | | | A |
| T | E | N | O | R |
| C | | | | T |
| H | E | A | T | H |

41 fruit, meat
42 draw, wear
43 read, eat
44 stars, crosses
45 hot, windy
46 5761
47 27651
48 562
49 5762
50 8651
51 evening, morning
52 ordinary, unusual
53 swift, steady
54 tilted, straight
55 ride, walk
56 9
57 3
58 y
59 p
60 n
61 s
62 d
63 trout
64 home
65 mist

## Paper 13

1–5 *Give one mark for each two correct answers:* bridge B, drill C, ferret A, baboon A, arcade B, rose D, cinema B, beige D, mole A, saw C
6 break, mend
7 stretch, shrink
8 empty, full
9 plentiful, scarce
10 winner, loser
11 b
12 e
13 s
14 y
15 t
16 stain
17 stead
18 tramp
19 ages
20 clean
21 alto
22 idea
23 hare
24 seas
25 tour
26 HEAR
27 FARM
28 BULK
29 WINE
30 SENT
31 sunny, woman, beach
32 spring, green, lambs
33 quickly, station, train
34 boat, rock, water
35 jumped, cold, swam
36 lie
37 pack
38 star
39 kind
40 cold
41–45

| B | R | A | V | E |
|---|---|---|---|---|
| I | | L | | A |
| S | I | T | E | S |
| O | | E | | E |
| N | | R | | L |

46 DP FU
47 8R 4T
48 CB FC
49 8A 5Z
50 FU EV
51 ❍ ◆ ❞ ①
52 ① ◆ ❍
53 TAG
54 TEA
55 GREAT
56 8945
57 31754
58 FACED
59 HEDGED
60 BEACH
61 act
62 belt
63 know
64 moor
65 sty

## Paper 14

1 appreciation, thanks
2 creak, squeak
3 gallant, brave
4 rubbish, litter
5 silence, quietness
6 n
7 r
8 d
9 m
10 d
11 even
12 deep
13 part
14 joyful
15 end
16 TRAP
17 TEAM
18 DRAG
19 STEM
20 PORT
21 nothing
22 carpet
23 landmark
24 another
25 bedstead
26 leap
27 skin
28 tall
29 farm
30 tool
31 BAKE
32 MARK
33 MAKE
34 LONG
35 COLT
36 borrow, you
37 shoes, are
38 one, buy
39 it, I'll

40 full, hope
41 finish, conclude
42 freeze, cool
43 second, minute
44 ebb, flow
45 noon, day
46 money
47 a lens
48 keys
49 a seat
50 child
51 ❞ ❍ ❍ ①
52 ① ❍ ◆ ①
53 GEAR
54 EAGER
55 GAVE
56 20
57 15
58 12
59 15
60 16
61 R
62 G
63 D
64 S
65 M

## Paper 15

1 summer, winter
2 newspapers, invitations
3 sings, reads
4 monkey, lion
5 flower, tree
6 front, back
7 rough, smooth
8 bent, straight
9 sell, buy
10 here, there
11 hose
12 raps
13 warm
14 this
15 seat
16 rain
17 fire
18 tooth
19 road
20 moon
21 news
22 then
23 hear
24 duet
25 fund
26 FREE
27 DEAD
28 ISLE
29 BRAT
30 BARK
31 street, you
32 wilting, hot
33 paper, used
34 blissfully, cat
35 in, sick
36 answer
37 find
38 study
39 believe
40 lengthy

41–45

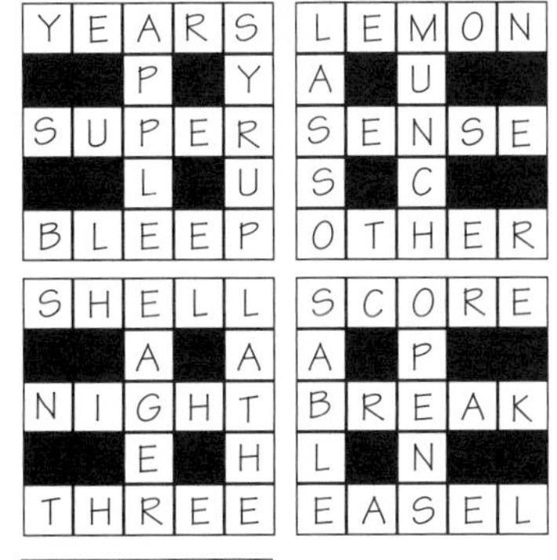

46 REASON
47 SCARED
48 DELIVER
49 CHASE
50 BOAST
51 1 ✦ 3 0 7
52 1 ✦ 4 3 △
53 △ 4 3 0
54 △ 3 0 7
55 0 4 3 1 ✦
56 k
57 b
58 e
59 n
60 l
61 bare
62 main
63 raft
64 cover
65 short

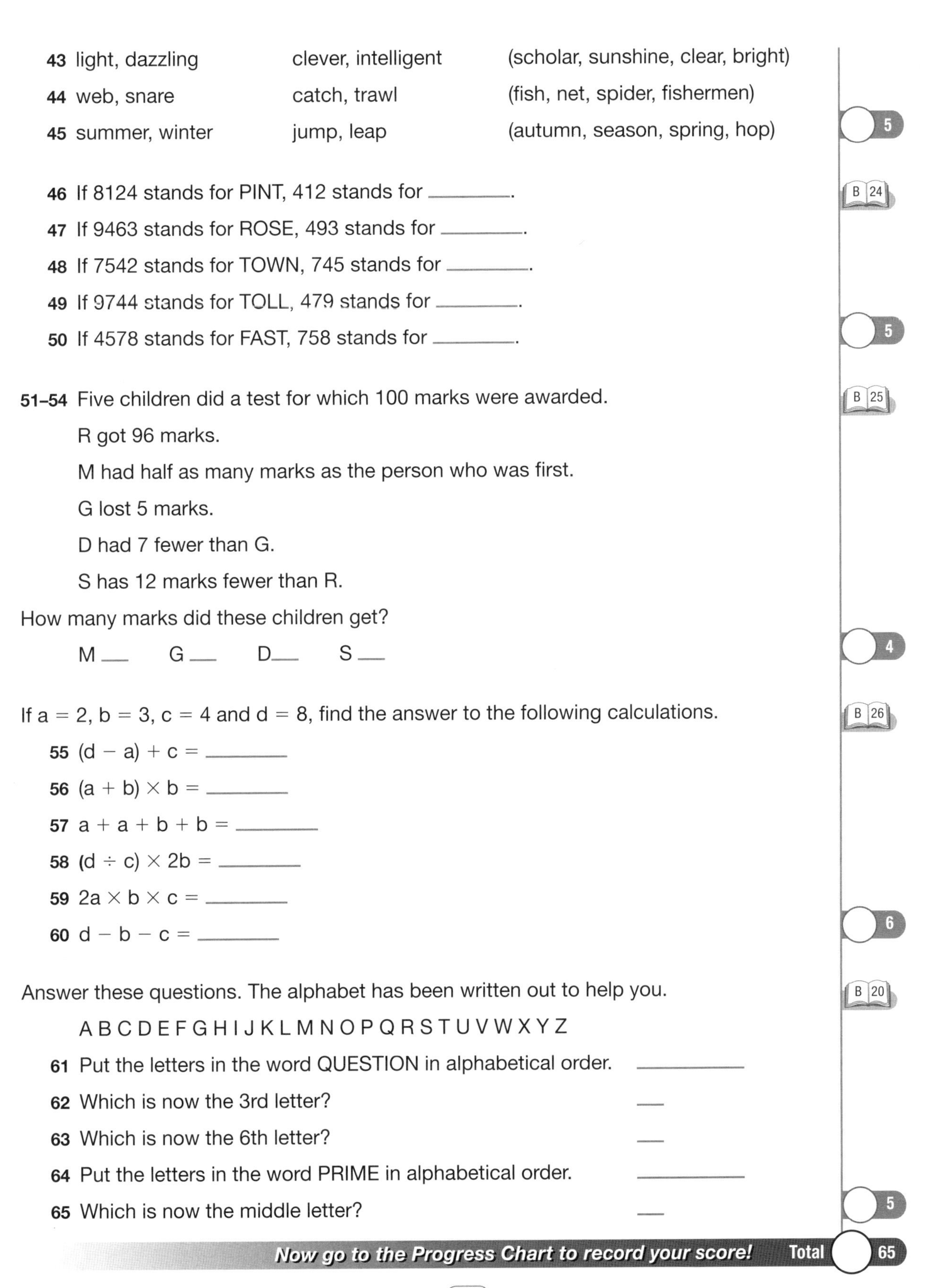

| | | | |
|---|---|---|---|
| **43** | light, dazzling | clever, intelligent | (scholar, sunshine, clear, bright) |
| **44** | web, snare | catch, trawl | (fish, net, spider, fishermen) |
| **45** | summer, winter | jump, leap | (autumn, season, spring, hop) |

5

B 24

**46** If 8124 stands for PINT, 412 stands for ________.

**47** If 9463 stands for ROSE, 493 stands for ________.

**48** If 7542 stands for TOWN, 745 stands for ________.

**49** If 9744 stands for TOLL, 479 stands for ________.

**50** If 4578 stands for FAST, 758 stands for ________.

5

B 25

**51–54** Five children did a test for which 100 marks were awarded.

R got 96 marks.

M had half as many marks as the person who was first.

G lost 5 marks.

D had 7 fewer than G.

S has 12 marks fewer than R.

How many marks did these children get?

M ___ G ___ D___ S ___

4

B 26

If a = 2, b = 3, c = 4 and d = 8, find the answer to the following calculations.

**55** $(d - a) + c =$ ________

**56** $(a + b) \times b =$ ________

**57** $a + a + b + b =$ ________

**58** $(d \div c) \times 2b =$ ________

**59** $2a \times b \times c =$ ________

**60** $d - b - c =$ ________

6

B 20

Answer these questions. The alphabet has been written out to help you.

A B C D E F G H I J K L M N O P Q R S T U V W X Y Z

**61** Put the letters in the word QUESTION in alphabetical order. ________

**62** Which is now the 3rd letter? ___

**63** Which is now the 6th letter? ___

**64** Put the letters in the word PRIME in alphabetical order. ________

**65** Which is now the middle letter? ___

5

***Now go to the Progress Chart to record your score!*** Total 65

# Paper 9

Find a word that is similar in meaning to the word in capital letters and that rhymes with the second word.

B 5

**Example** CABLE tyre wire

1 ELECTRICITY tower ______

2 SHORELINE toast ______

3 A LOT OF CATTLE word ______

4 PART OF A SHIRT dollar ______

5 TIMEPIECE mock ______

5

Rearrange the muddled letters in capitals to make a proper word. The answer will complete the sentence sensibly.

B 16

**Example** A BEZAR is an animal with stripes. ZEBRA

6 We spread TTREBU on bread. ______

7 Children often have BYRUGB knees! ______

8 The African LPHEEANT has big ears. ______

9 Put your TRELTI in the bin! ______

10 We put letters in NVEEESLOP. ______

5

Find the three-letter word which can be added to the letters in capitals to make a new word. The new word will complete the sentence sensibly.

B 22

**Example** The cat sprang onto the MO. USE

11 Please wash your HS before lunch. ______

12 The DPING tap kept me awake. ______

13 She is very NY and makes us laugh a lot. ______

14 It was much DER now that the lights had been turned off. ______

15 His HING was poor, he couldn't hear people talking. ______

5

Remove one letter from the word in capital letters to leave a new word. The meaning of the new word is given in the clue.

B 12

**Example** AUNT an insect ant

16 BEAT a flying mammal ______

17 COAST the price of something ______

18 FEVER always ______

19 PLANE window glass ______

20 SLING a musical sound made by a voice ______

5

Write the four-letter word hidden at the end of one word and the beginning of the next word. The order of the letters may not be changed.

**Example** The children had bats and balls. sand

21 Not only is the stamp attractive but it is also valuable. ______

22 It was the tallest tower ever seen. ______

23 My poor mother had four operations. ______

24 Izzy's rabbit chewed a hole in her hutch. ______

25 Well done, you're the last one out. ______

Move one letter from the first word and add it to the second word to make two new words.

**Example** hunt sip hut snip

| | | | |
|---|---|---|---|
| 26 bear | link | ______ | ______ |
| 27 plan | fit | ______ | ______ |
| 28 land | fake | ______ | ______ |
| 29 done | well | ______ | ______ |
| 30 stun | peal | ______ | ______ |

Complete the following sentences by selecting the most sensible word from each group of words given in the brackets. Underline the words selected.

**Example** The (children, books, foxes) carried the (houses, books, steps) home from the (greengrocer, library, factory).

31 Tim wears a black (shirt, handkerchief, scarf) when he plays (whist, football, scrabble) for the school (journey, team, work).

32 My pencil (grater, sharpener, cutter) is in my (cup, bed, bag) hanging on my (tree, floor, chair).

33 The (car, plane, ship) went into the (house, harbour, shed) very (slowly, cleverly, badly).

34 He (listened, watched, thought) very hard to (hear, catch, throw) the train (floating, going, coming) towards him.

35 In the (Sahara, Antarctic, jungle) icebergs are as (small, old, huge) as (penguins, garages, houses).

Find the missing number by using the two numbers outside the brackets in the same way as the other sets of numbers.

| | | | |
|---|---|---|---|
| **Example** | 2 [8] 4 | 3 [18] 6 | 5 [25] 5 |
| 36 | 11 [23] 12 | 6 [15] 9 | 18 [____] 11 |
| 37 | 6 [19] 25 | 7 [10] 17 | 9 [____] 23 |
| 38 | 7 [2] 14 | 11 [3] 33 | 6 [____] 6 |
| 39 | 3 [30] 5 | 7 [42] 3 | 6 [____] 2 |
| 40 | 8 [24] 3 | 6 [30] 5 | 9 [____] 8 |

Fill in the crosswords so that all the given words are included. You have been given one letter as a clue in each crossword.

41

stiff, none, meter, tense, fence

42

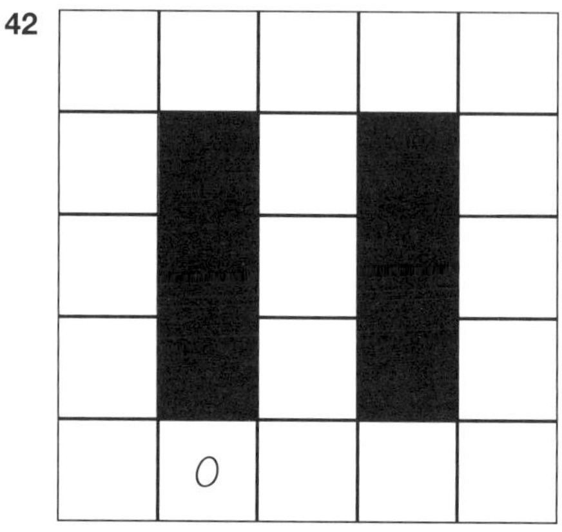


timer, torch, reach, treat, motor

43

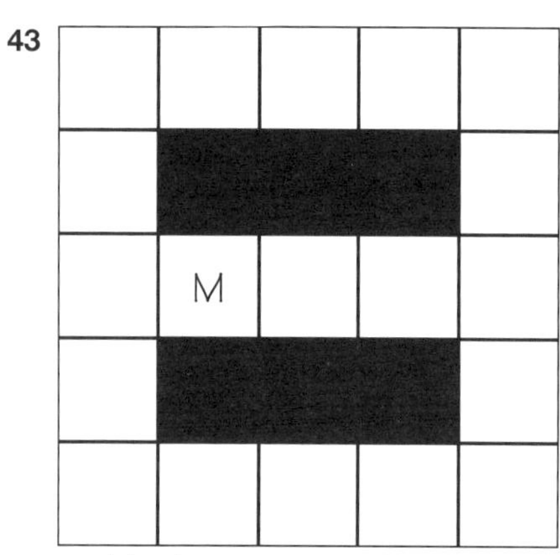


amble, horse, erect, heaps, sport

44

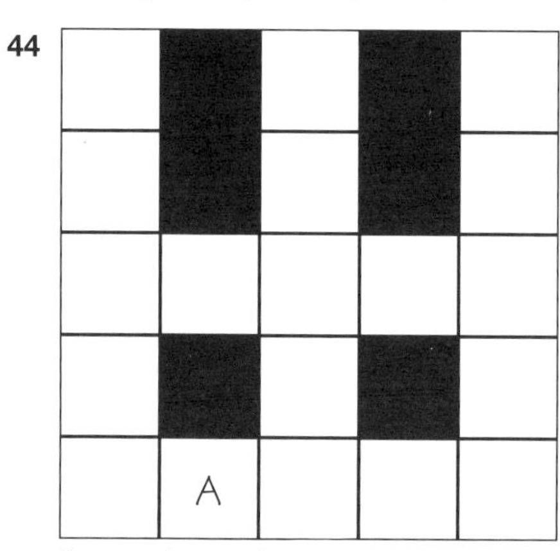


funny, layer, laser, towel, wands

45

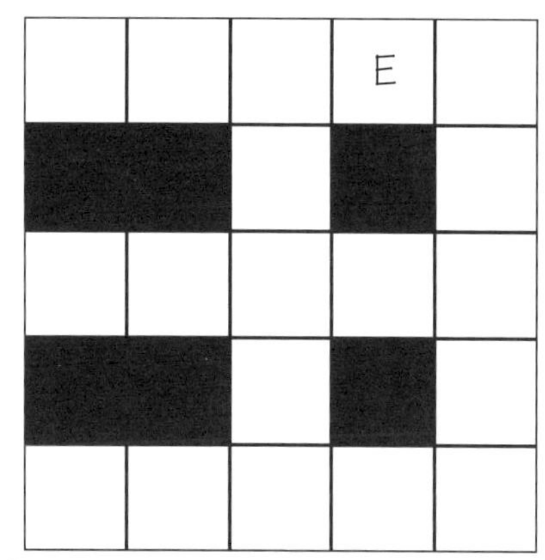


hover, nasty, steam, views, rummy

5

Rearrange the letters in capitals to make another word. The new word has something to do with the first two words.

B 16

**Example** spot soil SAINT STAIN

46 rock pebble NOTES ________

| | | | |
|---|---|---|---|
| **47** challenge | attempt | DEAR | ________ |
| **48** bush | plant | BRUSH | ________ |
| **49** box | container | TRACE | ________ |
| **50** end | back | RARE | ________ |

5

B 24

**51** If 2124 stands for PIPE, 214 stands for ________.

**52** If 2867 stands for LINK, 786 stands for ________.

**53** If 5234 stands for WEAR, 342 stands for ________.

**54** If 3216 stands for WRAP, 613 stands for ________.

**55** If 1729 stands for COAT, 219 stands for ________.

5

B 20

If these words were placed in alphabetical order, which word would come fourth?

| | | | | | |
|---|---|---|---|---|---|
| **56** lounge | locket | locals | loaded | lonely | ________ |
| **57** marry | blank | every | blown | march | ________ |

If these words were listed in reverse alphabetical order, which word would come second?

| | | | | | |
|---|---|---|---|---|---|
| **58** racket | raisin | raffle | rattle | rascal | ________ |
| **59** splint | spoken | square | superb | spread | ________ |
| **60** concert | foreign | collect | purpose | puppets | ________ |

5

B 25

**61–65** Six families live in South Street. From the information below, work out which family lives in which house and write them in on the chart.

| Browns | ________ | ________ |
|---|---|---|
| 1 | 3 | 5 |
| | SOUTH STREET | |
| 2 | 4 | 6 |
| ________ | ________ | ________ |

The Greys live between the Blacks and the Whites on the even side on South Street.

The Greens live opposite the Blacks.

The Browns live in Number 1.

The Blues live in a house with a higher number than the Whites.

5

***Now go to the Progress Chart to record your score!*** **Total** 65

# Paper 10

Underline the two words, one from each group, which are closest in meaning.

**Example** (race, shop, start) (finish, begin, end)

1 (choose, time, bend) (trick, open, curve)

2 (big, heavy, small) (old, slight, alike)

3 (create, ruin, ignore) (invite, call, destroy)

4 (author, book, story) (easel, painter, writer)

5 (run, travel, fast) (slow, carry, swift)

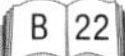

Find the three-letter word which can be added to the letters in capitals to make a new word. The new word will complete the sentence sensibly.

**Example** The cat sprang onto the MO. USE

6 We plant CABES in our vegetable garden each year. ________

7 The HST boy returned the wallet he found on the road. ________

8 'Take out some PR and a pencil,' said the teacher. ________

9 I like to have lettuce and TOOES in my salad. ________

10 My mum makes me hot tea with lemon when I have a sore THR. ________

Underline the one word which **can be made** from the letters of the word in capitals.

**Example** CHAMPION camping notch peach cramp chimp

| | | | | | | |
|---|---|---|---|---|---|---|
| 11 | HEAVE | head | have | vast | hive | hovel |
| 12 | BROTHER | another | there | broke | throb | bribe |
| 13 | FORCE | care | forge | core | fudge | free |
| 14 | GROPE | grape | rope | grip | rogue | pear |
| 15 | HANDS | shape | shore | ship | shade | sand |

Write the four-letter word hidden at the end of one word and the beginning of the next word. The order of the letters may not be changed.

**Example** The children had bats and balls. sand

16 I don't like the clothes in this shop. ________

17 The cinema shows new films each week. ________

18 Running around helps tire you out. ________

19 There's been an accident; come at once! ________

20 Jade received letters from people she had never heard of. ________

Move one letter from the first word and add it to the second word to make two new words.

B 13

**Example** hunt sip hut snip

21 fear can ______ ______

22 spoil eat ______ ______

23 hoist pant ______ ______

24 haunt lid ______ ______

25 drear spot ______ ______

5

Complete the following sentences by selecting the most sensible word from each group of words given in the brackets. Underline the words selected.

B 14

**Example** The (children, books, foxes) carried the (houses, books, steps) home from the (greengrocer, library, factory).

26 Jane has to go to the (house, cinema, school) as she has an (silly, important, small) exam and she (fears, hopes, wonders) if she will do well.

27 Luckily she (ate, found, read) her (umbrella, book, lunch) just before the (day, rain, bus) began.

28 In the event of a (silence, fire, flood) leave the (street, car, building) (slowly, badly, quickly).

29 I have lost my (ball, book, cat). She is (lazy, black, green) and has a (mouse, paw, collar).

30 He (ate, lost, drank) the lemonade quickly, (put on, took off, bought) his coat and (swam, ran, left).

5

Find and underline the two words which need to change places for the sentence to make sense.

B 17

**Example** She went to letter the write.

31 The better is weather now.

32 I'm supper forward to looking.

33 I like me book you gave the.

34 Up try to clean it do.

35 I vase over the knocked.

5

Fill in the missing letters and numbers.

B 23

**Example** AB is to CD as PQ is to RS.

36 A82 is to B81 as C80 is to ______.

37 D19 is to E19 as F20 is to ______.

38 C9 is to D12 as E15 is to ______.

39 AB5 is to CD6 as EF7 is to ______.

40 KLM is to MNO as OPQ is to ______.

5

Underline the two words, one from each group, which are most opposite in meaning.

**Example** (dawn, early, wake) (late, stop, sunrise)

41 (still, quiet, sudden) (motionless, active, silence)

42 (icy, freezing, warm) (cool, cold, frosty)

43 (bend, loosen, crack) (straighten, drop, catch)

44 (fix, trade, sell) (destroy, repair, improve)

45 (inside, low, between) (under, high, below)

B 9

5

Write these words backwards and put them in alphabetical order.

GAMBIT GARLAND GALLOP GAMBLE GATHER

________ ________ ________ ________ ________

46 Which is now the first word? ________

47 Which is now the middle word? ________

48 Which two letters are in all the words? ________

49 When the word is written forwards, which word has all the letters after the first in alphabetical order? ________

50 What is the total number of As in the words? __

B 20

5

If the code for DETAINS is ghbjklm, what are the codes for the following words?

51 NEAT ________

52 DENT ________

What do these codes stand for?

53 ghjl ________

54 mbjkl ________

B 24

4

Choose the word or phrase that makes the sentence true.

**Example** A LIBRARY always has (posters, a carpet, books, DVDs, stairs).

55 A PARTY always has (cake, music, gifts, guests, games).

56 A DOG always has a (lead, collar, kennel, tag, coat).

57 A RESTAURANT always has (food, a patio, music, tablecloths, candles).

58 A CAR always has (passengers, air conditioning, a radio, a clock, a steering wheel).

59 A BOARD GAME always has (dice, rules, cards, a timer, a scorecard).

B 14

5

Choose two words, one from each set of brackets, to complete the sentence in the best way.

B 15

**Example** Tall is to (tree, short, colour) as narrow is to (thin, white, wide).

60 Combine is to (leave, destroy, add) as subtract is to (cover, move, reduce).

61 Fail is to (lose, try, play) as draw is to (tie, improve, succeed).

62 Trap is to (catch, deliver, ignore) as release is to (free, lose, protect).

63 Donate is to (charge, win, give) as receive is to (accept, present, sell).

64 Order is to (choose, command, use) as ask is to (answer, request, refuse).

65 Erase is to (delete, highlight, insert) as ring is to (circle, finger, hoop).

6

*Now go to the Progress Chart to record your score!* Total 65

# Paper 11

Underline the two words in each line which are most similar in type or meaning.

B 5

| | | | | | |
|---|---|---|---|---|---|
| **Example** | dear | pleasant | poor | extravagant | expensive |
| 1 | hot | cold | shout | wet | yell |
| 2 | go | frighten | need | calm | require |
| 3 | bench | tape | parcel | mail | chair |
| 4 | show | light | ask | day | enquire |
| 5 | open | stand | close | sit | shut |

5

Find the three-letter word which can be added to the letters in capitals to make a new word. The new word will complete the sentence sensibly.

B 22

**Example** The cat sprang onto the MO. USE

6 He bought an EXSIVE car. ______

7 The cup SMED on the floor. ______

8 Next month will be MH. ______

9 The car was driven BACKDS. ______

10 He SPED on the icy road. ______

5

If the letters in the following words were arranged in alphabetical order, which letter would come in the middle?

B 20

11 baron ___

12 night ___

13 earth ___

14 youth ___

15 torch ___

5

Find a word that can be put in front of each of the following words to make new, compound words.

B 11

**Example** cast fall ward pour *down*

**16** storm ball plough man ________

**17** out book cuff shake ________

**18** fall proof tight colour ________

**19** ground line stand arm ________

**20** where one time how ________

Write the four-letter word hidden at the end of one word and the beginning of the next word. The order of the letters may not be changed.

**Example** The children had bats and balls. *sand*

**21** The approach to the school is busy. ________

**22** Each pair is different. ________

**23** He started school when he was five years old. ________

**24** There was no need for you to cry. ________

**25** It is nice when we are here on time. ________

Change the first word into the last word by changing one letter at a time and making a new, different word in the middle.

**Example** CASE *CASH* LASH

**26** STAY ________ SLAM

**27** THAT ________ CHAP

**28** CAST ________ PASS

**29** FIRE ________ DIRT

**30** DUCK ________ LACK

Find and underline the two words which need to change places for the sentence to make sense.

**Example** She went to <u>letter</u> the <u>write</u>.

**31** New is your which house?

**32** The wet is awfully towel.

**33** Do borrow want to you it?

**34** She very it was said interesting.

**35** I cover the picture on the like.

5

Change one word so that the sentence makes sense. Underline the word you are taking out and write your new word on the line.

B 14

**Example** I waited in line to buy a <u>book</u> to see the film. *ticket*

**36** The alphabet has 26 different numbers. __________

**37** A torch can help you see in the light. __________

**38** An aeroplane can run to other countries. __________

**39** Using a skipping string can keep you fit. __________

**40** Peas, beans and carrots are all flowers. __________

5

Fill in the crosswords so that all the given words are included. You have been given one letter as a clue in each crossword.

**41**

treat, unfit, field, until, laden

**42**

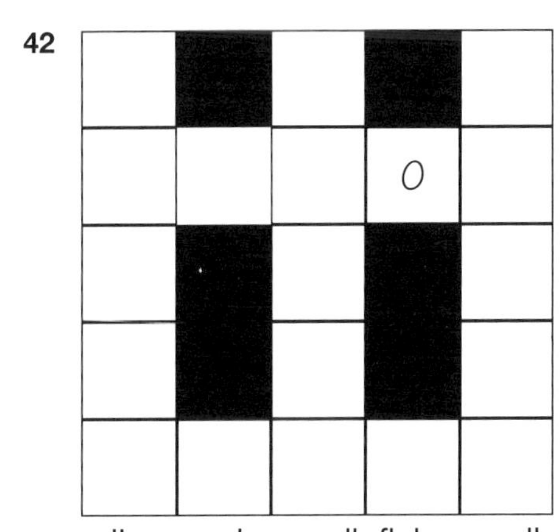


allow, parks, spell, flake, swell

**43**

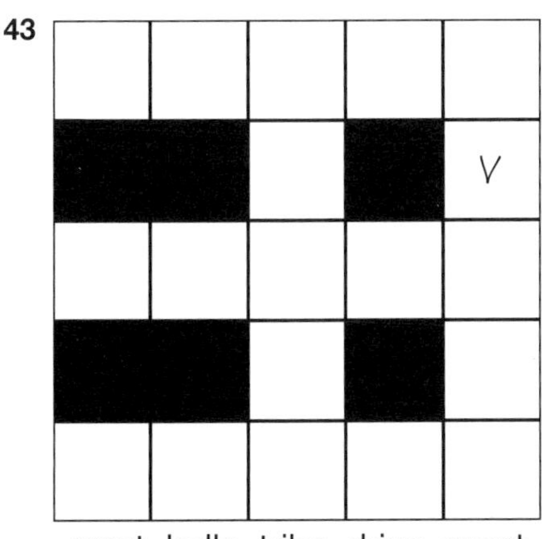


great, ladle, tribe, drive, event

**44**

crate, other, beach, robes, spear

45

ankle, super, usual, spoke, creek

5

Give the two missing groups of letters and numbers in the following sequences. The alphabet has been written out to help you.

B 23

A B C D E F G H I J K L M N O P Q R S T U V W X Y Z

| | | | | | | |
|---|---|---|---|---|---|---|
| **Example** | CQ | DP | EQ | FP | GQ | HP |
| **46** | BK | BL | CM | ___ | ___ | DP |
| **47** | 2P | ___ | 8T | 11V | 14X | ___ |
| **48** | ___ | YB | XC | ___ | VE | UF |
| **49** | WV | XT | ___ | ZP | ___ | BL |
| **50** | DCB | EDC | FED | ___ | ___ | IHG |

5

Rearrange the letters in capitals to make another word. The new word has something to do with the first two words.

B 16

| | | | | |
|---|---|---|---|---|
| **Example** | spot | soil | SAINT | STAIN |
| **51** | cut | rip | RATE | ________ |
| **52** | nuisance | annoyance | PETS | ________ |
| **53** | food | dinner | MALE | ________ |
| **54** | pipe | tube | SHOE | ________ |
| **55** | whiskers | moustache | BREAD | ________ |

5

If a = 2, b = 3, c = 4, d = 5, f = 6, g = 7, find the answer to the following calculations.

B 26

**56** abc = ___ **57** bcd = ___

2

Solve the problems by working out the letter codes. The alphabet has been written out to help you.

B 24

A B C D E F G H I J K L M N O P Q R S T U V W X Y Z

**Example** In a code, SECOND is written as UGEQPF. How would you write THIRD? VJKTF

**58** In a code, FLOWER is written as DJMUCP. How would you write LOW? ________

**59** In a code, RUN is written as TWP. What does mean PWV mean? ________

60 In a code, JUMP is written as ITLO. What does ETM mean? ________

61 In a code, DUCK is written as CTBJ. How would you write NEXT? ________

62 In a code, ROSE is written as SPTF. How would you write HOLIDAY? ________

5

Find a word that is similar in meaning to the word in capital letters and that rhymes with the second word.

B 5

| | | | |
|---|---|---|---|
| **Example** | CABLE | tyre | wire |
| 63 | GROUP | stand | ________ |
| 64 | UNEVEN | cuff | ________ |
| 65 | NOT SOUR | bleat | ________ |

3

***Now go to the Progress Chart to record your score!*** Total 65

# Paper 12

Underline the two words which are the odd ones out in the following groups of words.

B 4

**Example** black <u>king</u> purple green <u>house</u>

| | | | | | |
|---|---|---|---|---|---|
| 1 | skip | lead | walk | run | iron |
| 2 | river | mountain | ocean | sea | hill |
| 3 | cross | kind | generous | angry | loving |
| 4 | red | sun | blue | moon | green |
| 5 | sunny | rest | warm | sleep | fine |

5

Find the three-letter word which can be added to the letters in capitals to make a new word. The new word will complete the sentence sensibly.

B 22

**Example** The cat sprang onto the MO. USE

6 It was so cold it was SING. ________

7 The king shouted for his SERT. ________

8 He woke LY that morning. ________

9 She picked some PROSES in the wood. ________

10 The dog gave him a nasty SCCH. ________

5

Underline two words, one from each group, that go together to form a new word. The word in the first group always comes first.

B 8

**Example** (hand, green, for) (light, house, sure)

11 (red, green, blue) (fingers, bell, rose)

12 (sun, light, bright) (rub, off, shine)

13 (short, tall, foot) (step, sure, arm)

14 (now, after, before) (wards, went, down)

15 (short, foot, hurt) (good, goal, ball)

5

Write the four-letter word hidden at the end of one word and the beginning of the next word. The order of the letters may not be changed.

B 21

**Example** The children had bats and balls. sand

16 My mother makes us keep our house tidy. ______

17 I like juice made from tropical fruits. ______

18 Each apple costs forty-nine pence. ______

19 After all those years, I was still interested in it. ______

20 Despite losing I don't regret changing. ______

5

Move one letter from the first word and add it to the second word to make two new words.

B 13

**Example** hunt sip hut snip

21 steam key ______ ______

22 float her ______ ______

23 stall kin ______ ______

24 bread foe ______ ______

25 print ate ______ ______

5

Complete the following sentences by selecting the most sensible word from each group of words given in the brackets. Underline the words selected.

B 14

**Example** The (children, books, foxes) carried the (houses, books, steps) home from the (greengrocer, library, factory).

26 She (tried, worked, walked) to get her (son, dog, daughter) to do his (radio, drink, homework).

27 The (number, letter, sign) at the end of the (road, word, sum) says (come, run, stop).

28 The (ship, plane, car) in the (lane, sea, sky) is (driving, flying, sailing) very high.

29 We (swum, walked, skipped) as (slowly, lazily, fast) as we could to get to the (castle, cloud, friend) before dark.

30 The (police, villagers, highwaymen) stopped the (canoe, cart, coach) and stole the travellers' (food, shoes, gold).

5

Fill in the missing letters. The alphabet has been written out to help you.

B 23

A B C D E F G H I J K L M N O P Q R S T U V W X Y Z

**Example** AB is to CD as PQ is to RS.

31 AC is to EG as JL is to ______.

32 AB is to WX as CD is to ______.

33 ACE is to BDF as LNP is to ______.

34 AZ is to BY as CX is to ______.

35 ACB is to BCA as EGF is to ______.

Fill in the crosswords so that all the given words are included. You have been given one letter as a clue in each crossword.

B 19

36

anvil, orbit, brave,
tails, organ

37

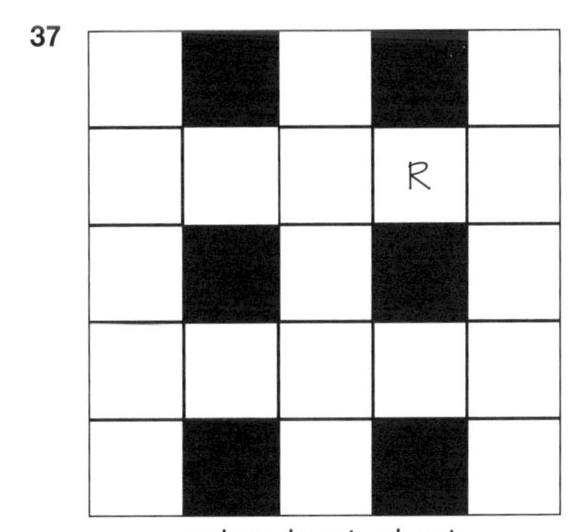


ochre, least, chest,
ports, tusks

38

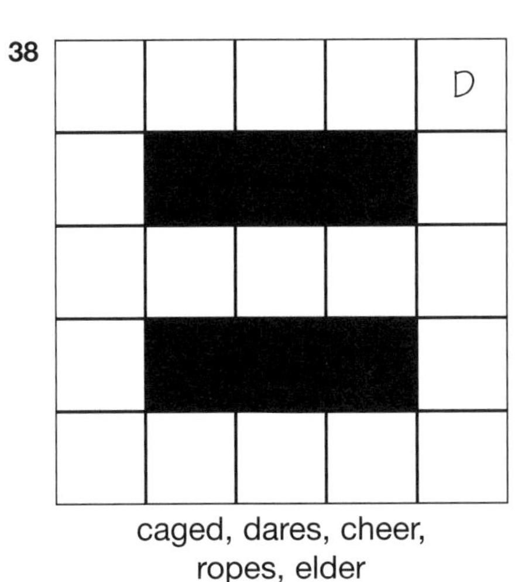


caged, dares, cheer,
ropes, elder

39

S

punch, sighs, husks,
sates, night

**40**

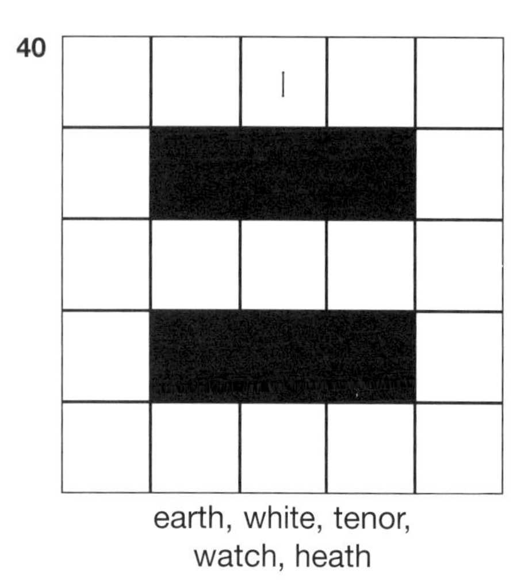


earth, white, tenor,
watch, heath

5

B 14

Change one word so that the sentence makes sense. Underline the word you are taking out and write your new word on the line.

**Example** I waited in line to buy a book to see the film. *ticket*

**41** If you don't eat fish or fruit you are a vegetarian. ___________

**42** In a car you should always draw a seat belt. ___________

**43** In Chinese restaurants many people read with chopsticks. ___________

**44** Noughts and stars is a fun game to play with friends. ___________

**45** It was so hot last night that a tree in our garden was blown over. ___________

5

B 24

Here are the number codes for four words. Match the right word to the right code.

| SHOE | SOW | ROSE | WHOSE | SHOW |
|---|---|---|---|---|
| 5 7 6 2 | 5 7 6 1 | 2 7 6 5 1 | 8 6 5 1 | 5 6 2 |

**46** SHOE ________ **47** WHOSE ________

**48** SOW ________ **49** SHOW ________

**50** ROSE ________

5

B 15

Choose two words, one from each set of brackets, to complete the sentences in the best way.

**Example** Tall is to (tree, short, colour) as narrow is to (thin, white, wide).

**51** Dusk is to (evening, dark, moon) as dawn is to (sunset, night, morning).

**52** Common is to (few, ordinary, lost) as unique is to (unusual, broken, expensive).

**53** Sudden is to (skilled, quiet, swift) as gradual is to (steady, new, careless).

**54** Leaning is to (tilted, standing, thin) as upright is to (straight, fallen, lying).

**55** Horse is to (ride, saddle, hoof) as dog is to (bone, walk, pet).

5

If a = 2, b = 3, c = 4, d = 5, find the answer to the following calculations.

B 26

**56** $a + b + c =$ ________

**57** $(c + d) \div b =$ ________

2

Find the letter which will complete both pairs of words, ending the first word and starting the second. The same letter must be used for both pairs of words.

B 10

**Example** mea ( t ) able fi ( t ) ub

**58** man ( __ ) awn da ( __ ) et

**59** tra ( __ ) ea ho ( __ ) it

**60** daw ( __ ) ote mai ( __ ) un

**61** pas ( __ ) aw wa ( __ ) ty

**62** bea ( __ ) ry be ( __ ) ew

5

Find a word that is similar in meaning to the word in capital letters and that rhymes with the second word.

B 5

**Example** CABLE tyre wire

**63** A FISH spout ________

**64** HOUSE comb ________

**65** FOG hissed ________

3

***Now go to the Progress Chart to record your score!*** **Total** 65

# Paper 13

**1–5** Look at these groups of words.

B 1

| A | B | C | D |
|---|---|---|---|
| mule | theatre | spanner | purple |
| monkey | town hall | anvil | pink |

Choose the correct group for each of the words below. Write in the letter.

bridge __ drill __ ferret __ baboon __

arcade __ rose __ cinema __ beige __

mole __ saw __

5

Underline the two words, one from each group, which are the most opposite in meaning.

B 9

**Example** (dawn, early, wake) (late, stop, sunrise)

6 (break, whole, part) (mend, fast, heal)

7 (long, land, stretch) (length, measure, shrink)

8 (heat, empty, weight) (bottom, full, light)

9 (drop, lots, plentiful) (hold, scarce, scare)

10 (fight, top, winner) (left, loser, first)

5

Find the letter which will end the first word and start the second word.

B 10

**Example** peac ( h ) ome

11 num ( __ ) read 12 pip ( __ ) ver 13 tos ( __ ) oak

14 pla ( __ ) ell 15 tha ( __ ) int

5

Underline the one word which **cannot be made** from the letters of the word in capital letters.

B 7

| | | | | | | |
|---|---|---|---|---|---|---|
| **Example** | STATIONERY | stone | tyres | ration | nation | noisy |
| 16 | TERRACE | care | rate | stain | trace | crate |
| 17 | DISTANT | stead | stand | stint | ants | dint |
| 18 | PAINTER | trip | rain | tramp | nape | print |
| 19 | GENERAL | large | near | rage | gear | ages |
| 20 | CLEAREST | clean | real | star | race | steer |

5

Write the four-letter word hidden at the end of one word and the beginning of the next word. The order of the letters may not be changed.

B 21

**Example** The children had bats and balls. sand

21 Going to the seaside is an ideal tonic. ________

22 The cup is beside a bunch of flowers. ________

23 Her teeth are white and beautifully clean. ________

24 It means it is easy to control. ________

25 We think that our ways are best. ________

5

Change the first word into the last word by changing one letter at a time and making a new, different word in the middle.

B 13

**Example** CASE CASH LASH

26 GEAR ________ HEAL 27 FIRM ________ HARM

28 BULB ________ SULK 29 WISE ________ WANE

30 SEAT ________ SEND

5

Complete the following sentences by selecting the most sensible word from each group of words given in the brackets. Underline the words selected.

B 14

**Example** The (children, books, foxes) carried the (houses, books, steps) home from the (greengrocer, library, factory).

**31** The day was (frosty, sunny, raining) and the (dog, woman, baby) went to sunbathe at the (town, slopes, beach).

**32** It was (spring, summer, autumn), the trees were (brown, dead, green) and the (toads, birds, lambs) were in the fields.

**33** We ran (yesterday, tomorrow, quickly) to the (house, shop, station) as we didn't want to miss the (truck, bike, train).

**34** The (wheelbarrow, boat, tree) hit the (rock, grass, rain) so hard that (water, ice, birds) came on board.

**35** We (ran, walked, jumped) overboard. The water was (dirty, muddy, cold) but we warmed up as we (drank, swam, ate).

5

Underline the one word in the brackets which will go equally well with both the pairs of words outside the brackets.

B 5

| | | | |
|---|---|---|---|
| **Example** | rush, attack | cost, fee | (price, hasten, strike, charge, money) |
| **36** | untruth, false | rest, lounge | (sleep, invent, fall, lie, support) |
| **37** | group, gang | fill, box | (tie, luggage, pack, carry, crate) |
| **38** | planet, sun | performer, celebrity | (moon, sky, actor, hero, star) |
| **39** | considerate, nice | type, sort | (gentle, kind, set, class, friendly) |
| **40** | cool, chilly | flu, infection | (freezing, sneeze, illness, cold, icy) |

5

Fill in the crosswords so that all the given words are included. You have been given one letter as a clue in each crossword.

**41**

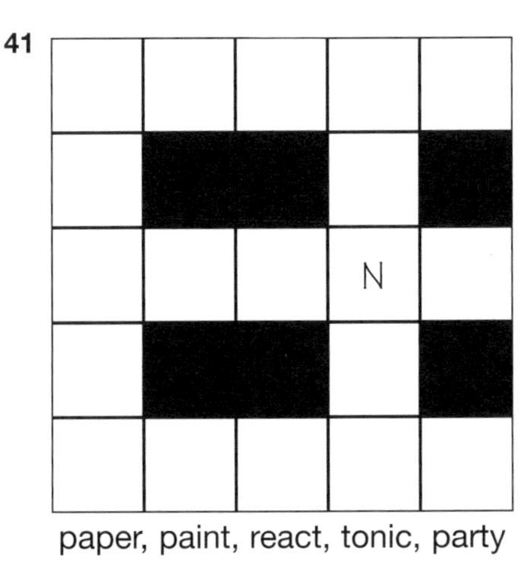


paper, paint, react, tonic, party

**42**

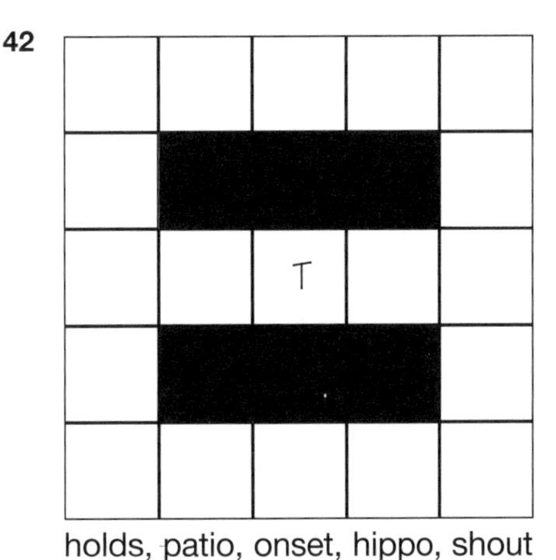


holds, patio, onset, hippo, shout

43

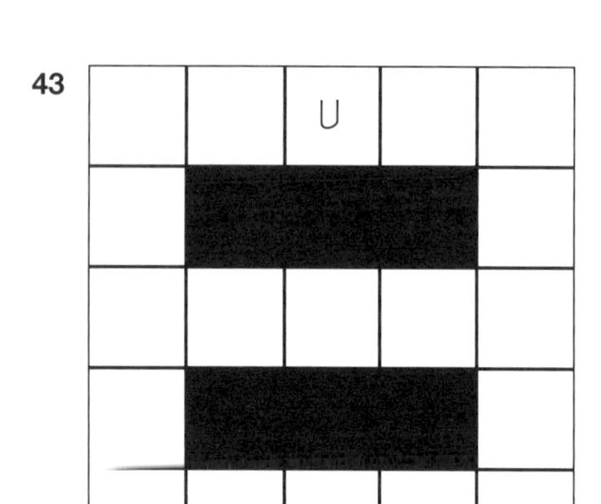


knots, pluck, hoops, perch, radio

44

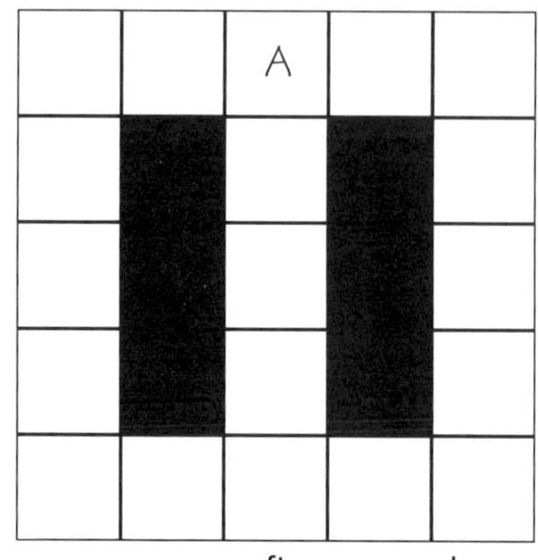


craze, error, after, rarer, clear

45

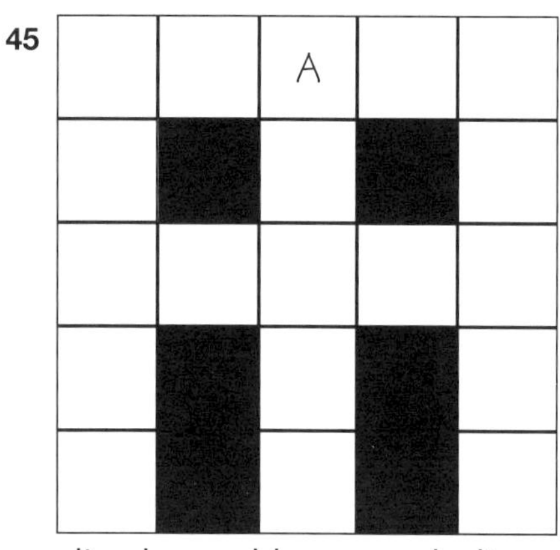


alter, brave, bison, easel, sites

5

Give the two missing groups of letters and numbers in the following sequences. The alphabet has been written out to help you.

B 23

A B C D E F G H I J K L M N O P Q R S T U V W X Y Z

| | | | | | | |
|---|---|---|---|---|---|---|
| **Example** | CQ | DP | EQ | FP | GQ | HP |
| **46** | ___ | EQ | FR | DS | ET | ___ |
| **47** | 128J | 64L | 32N | 16P | ___ | ___ |
| **48** | AA | BA | ___ | DB | EC | ___ |
| **49** | 8C | 5B | ___ | ___ | 8Y | 5X |
| **50** | ___ | ___ | DW | CX | BY | AZ |

5

If the code for GRATE is △ ❍ ◆ ❞ ①, what are the codes for the following words?

B 24

**51** RATE ________ **52** EAR ________

What do these codes stand for?

**53** ❞ ◆ △ ________

**54** ❞ ① ◆ ________

**55** △ ❍ ① ◆ ❞ ________

5

The first 10 letters of the alphabet are written as the first 10 numbers, i.e. A = 1 B = 2 etc.

B 24

Write these as numbers.

**56** HIDE ________ **57** CAGED ________

What are these words?

**58** 61354 ________ **59** 854754 ________ **60** 25138 ________

5

Underline the word in each line that has its letters in alphabetical order.

B 20

| | | | | |
|---|---|---|---|---|
| **61** word | act | letter | seen | frog |
| **62** omelette | gasp | belt | through | under |
| **63** know | gain | team | soon | from |
| **64** spoon | pram | night | brag | moor |
| **65** slice | peach | dunk | sty | frail |

5

***Now go to the Progress Chart to record your score!*** **Total** 65

# Paper 14

Underline the pair of words most similar in meaning.

B 5

**Example** come, go <u>roam, wander</u> fear, fare

| | | |
|---|---|---|
| **1** appreciation, thanks | please, prize | gale, calm |
| **2** present, past | paper, bins | creak, squeak |
| **3** unknown, famous | gallant, brave | soap, brush |
| **4** rubbish, litter | noun, verb | noisy, quiet |
| **5** hour, time | silence, quietness | dust, polish |

5

Find the letter which will end the first word and start the second word.

B 10

**Example** peac ( <u>h</u> ) ome

**6** whe ( __ ) ettle **7** fea ( __ ) ubber

**8** swor ( __ ) elight **9** ste ( __ ) ount

**10** soun ( __ ) awn

5

Underline one word in the brackets which is most opposite in meaning to the word in capitals.

B 6

**Example** WIDE (broad vague long <u>narrow</u> motorway)

**11** ODD (peculiar queer strange even unjust)

**12** SHALLOW (deep water dive puddle shape)

| | | |
|---|---|---|
| **13** | WHOLE | (complete part some never here) |
| **14** | SAD | (miserable joyful sorry hopeless hateful) |
| **15** | START | (begin open commence end first) |

5

B 18

Look at the first group of three words. The word in the middle has been made from the other two words. Complete the second group of three words in the same way, making a new word in the middle.

| | | | | | | |
|---|---|---|---|---|---|---|
| **Example** | PAIN | INTO | TOOK | ALSO | SOON | ONLY |
| **16** | COMB | BALE | ALES | PART | ______ | RAPS |
| **17** | WIDE | DESK | SKIP | SITE | ______ | AMPS |
| **18** | OPEN | NOSE | SENT | RAID | ______ | AGUE |
| **19** | SAGE | GETS | TEST | MAST | ______ | TONE |
| **20** | FREE | REEL | SEAL | SPOT | ______ | FRET |

5

B 8

Underline two words, one from each group, that go together to form a new word. The word in the first group always comes first.

| | | |
|---|---|---|
| **Example** | (hand, green, for) | (light, house, sure) |
| **21** | (no, two, duet) | (end, here, thing) |
| **22** | (drive, steer, car) | (hat, road, pet) |
| **23** | (land, earth, sky) | (mark, road, way) |
| **24** | (how, an, why) | (self, other, is) |
| **25** | (cot, bed, sleep) | (stead, stroll, stand) |

5

B 21

Write the four-letter word hidden at the end of one word and the beginning of the next word. The order of the letters may not be changed.

**Example** The children had bats and balls. sand

**26** A single apple is very good for you. ______

**27** This kind of behaviour is useless. ______

**28** To speak like that isn't allowed. ______

**29** You will need to write that far more neatly. ______

**30** Come quickly or you will be too late. ______

5

B 13

Change the first word into the last word by changing one letter at a time and making a new, different word in the middle.

**Example** CASE CASH LASH

**31** FAKE ______ BALE

**32** LARK ______ MARE

33 MADE ________ CAKE

34 SONG ________ LONE

35 COLD ________ COOT

5

Find and underline the two words which need to change places for the sentence to make sense.

B 17

**Example** She went to letter the write.

36 Do borrow want to you it?

37 Where shoes your are?

38 I must one a new buy.

39 It clean I'll tomorrow.

40 I full I'll get hope marks.

5

Choose two words, one from each set of brackets, to complete the sentence in the best way.

B 23

**Example** Smile is to happiness as (drink, tear, shout) is to (whisper, laugh, sorrow).

41 Depart is to leave as (change, ignore, finish) is to (remain, begin, conclude).

42 Heat is to warm as (wash, freeze, chop) is to (cool, boil, bake).

43 Pence is to pound as (second, day, month) is to (minute, century, decade).

44 Find is to lose as (easy, earth, ebb) is to (sun, flow, world).

45 Midnight is to night as (evening, noon, night) is to (day, dawn, winter).

5

Choose the word or phrase that makes the sentence true.

B 14

**Example** A LIBRARY always has (posters, a carpet, books, DVDs, stairs).

46 A BANK always has (sweets, music, coffee, money, a guard).

47 A CAMERA always has (film, a strap, a case, a lens, a stand).

48 A PIANO always has (keys, music, a music stand, a seat, a clock).

49 A CHAIR always has (wheels, arms, a cushion, a seat, a footrest).

50 A FATHER always has a (wife, hobby, child, car, daughter).

5

If the code for AVERAGE is ◆ ❞ ❍ ① ◆ △ ❍, what are the codes for the following words?

B 24

51 VEER ________ 52 REAR ________

What do these codes stand for?

53 △ ❍ ◆ ① ________ 54 ❍ ◆ △ ❍ ① ________

55 △ ◆ ❞ ❍ ________

5

If A = 1, B = 2, C = 3, D = 4, E = 5, F = 6, find the sum of these words.

B 26

**56** F + E + E + D = ___ **57** C + A + F + E = ___

**58** B + E + A + D = ___ **59** F + A + C + E = ___

**60** D + E + A +F = ___

5

Five children did a test for which 100 marks were awarded. R lost 4 marks, M had half as many marks as the person who came top, G lost 5 marks, D had 7 marks fewer than G and S had 12 marks fewer than R.

B 25

**61** Who came top? ___ **62** Who was 2nd? ___

**63** Who came 3rd? ___ **64** Who came 4th? ___

**65** Who came 5th? ___

5

***Now go to the Progress Chart to record your score!*** **Total** 65

# Paper 15

Change one word so that the sentence makes sense. Underline the word you are taking out and write your new word on the line.

B 14

**Example** I waited in line to buy a <u>book</u> to see the film. *ticket*

**1** Summer is my favourite season because I love it when it snows. ______

**2** I sent out newspapers to everyone I wanted to come to my birthday party. ______

**3** My mother sings out a story to me before bed each night. ______

**4** The monkey is known as the king of the jungle. ______

**5** Elm, oak and maple are all types of flower. ______

5

Underline the pair of words most opposite in meaning.

B 9

**Example** cup, mug coffee, milk <u>hot, cold</u>

| | | | |
|---|---|---|---|
| **6** | conceal, hide | front, back | modern, new |
| **7** | rough, smooth | rapid, quick | hope, help |
| **8** | tested, tried | bent, straight | gap, hole |
| **9** | stern, strict | ally, friend | sell, buy |
| **10** | here, there | show, display | angry, cross |

5

Remove two letters from the word in capital letters to leave a new word. The meaning of the new word is given in the clue.

B 12

**Example** MONKEY lives in a monastery monk

11 HOUSES tube ______

12 GRAPES knocks ______

13 SWARMS not cool ______

14 THINGS not that ______

15 SHEATH chair ______

5

Find a word that can be put in front of each of the following words to make new, compound words.

B 11

| | | | | | |
|---|---|---|---|---|---|
| **Example** | cast | fall | ward | pour | down |
| 16 | bow | drop | fall | coat | ______ |
| 17 | guard | fly | work | place | ______ |
| 18 | ache | brush | paste | pick | ______ |
| 19 | show | works | block | worthy | ______ |
| 20 | struck | beam | light | stone | ______ |

5

Write the four-letter word hidden at the end of one word and the beginning of the next word. The order of the letters may not be changed.

B 21

**Example** The children had bats and balls. sand

21 For his birthday, I got Dad new socks. ______

22 The next time he snaps, I'm going! ______

23 The art teacher was unwell today. ______

24 She missed her turn due to long queues. ______

25 Areas of path on the cliff under our feet were slippery. ______

5

Look at the first group of three words. The word in the middle has been made from the other two words. Complete the second group of three words in the same way, making a new word in the middle of the group.

B 18

| | | | | | | |
|---|---|---|---|---|---|---|
| **Example** | PAIN | INTO | TOOK | ALSO | SOON | ONLY |
| 26 | CODE | COST | FAST | FROG | ______ | GLEE |
| 27 | DECK | KICK | SICK | KIND | ______ | LEAD |

| | | | | | | |
|---|---|---|---|---|---|---|
| **28** OPEN | PETS | POTS | DISK | ______ | ABLE |
| **29** CLAP | PLAN | NAPE | CRAB | ______ | TASK |
| **30** SLIP | PILL | LOUD | DRAB | ______ | KNOW |

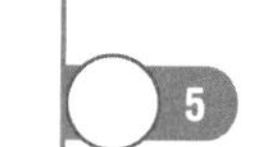

Find and underline the two words which need to change places for the sentence to make sense.

**Example** She went to letter the write.

**31** Do Street live on the High you?

**32** It is wilting and the flowers are hot.

**33** I've paper all the used already.

**34** The blissfully slept cat in the sun.

**35** I feel in sick a car.

Underline the word in the brackets closest in meaning to the word in capitals.

**Example** UNHAPPY (unkind death laughter sad friendly)

**36** REPLY (question comment answer write explain)

**37** DISCOVER (lose hide lock borrow find)

**38** EXAMINE (own paint fix study trick)

**39** TRUST (win believe pay stop consider)

**40** LONG (short small lengthy light thin)

Fill in the crosswords so that all the given words are included. You have been given one letter as a clue in each crossword.

**41**

apple, super, years, syrup, bleep

**42**

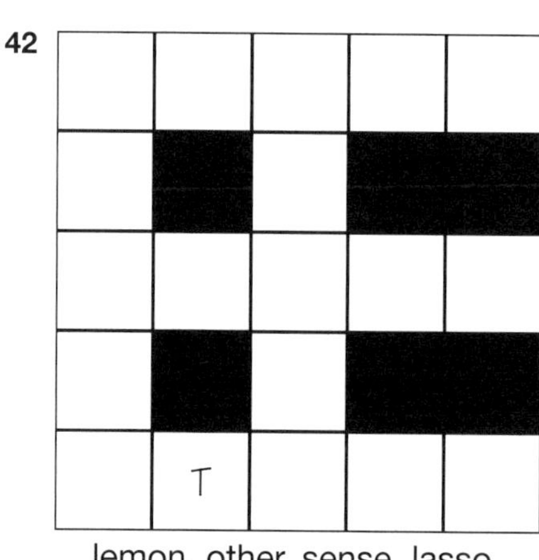


lemon, other, sense, lasso, munch

**43**

eager, night, shell, three, lathe

**44**

break, opens, score, sable, easel

**45**

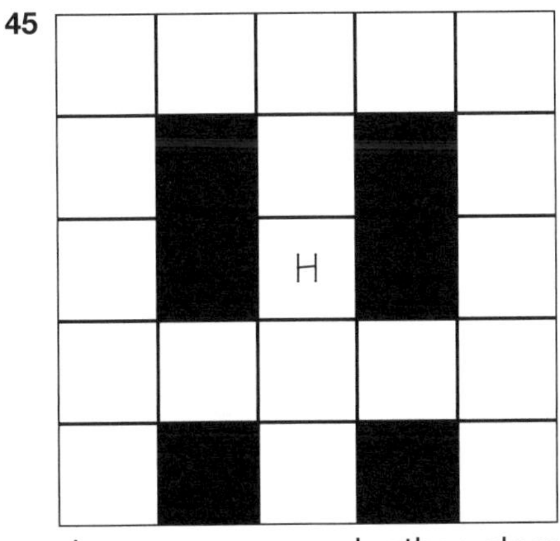


drear, arena, crowd, other, clear

5

B 20

In each line underline the word which would come in the middle if the words were arranged in alphabetical order.

**46** RECKON REASON REBEL READY REALISE

**47** SCHEME SAILOR SCENE SCARED SAFETY

**48** DEPRESS DELETE DEPEND DELIGHT DELIVER

**49** CLOSE CHASE CLIFF CHAOS CHART

**50** BOILING BRAWL BLANK BOAST BLARE

5

B 24

Here are the codes for five words. Match the right word to the right code.

| CHART | CHEAP | PEAR | PART | REACH |
|---|---|---|---|---|
| △ 4 3 0 | △ 3 0 7 | 0 4 3 1 ✦ | 1 ✦ 4 3 △ | 1 ✦ 3 0 7 |

**51** CHART ________ **52** CHEAP ________

**53** PEAR ________ **54** PART ________

**55** REACH ________

5

Find the letter which will complete both pairs of words, ending the first word and starting the second. The same letter must be used for both pairs of words.

B 10

**Example** mea ( t ) able fi ( t ) ub

56 drin ( __ ) now flic ( __ ) ite

57 stu ( __ ) un fla ( __ ) at

58 til ( __ ) yes slim ( __ ) nds

59 wor ( __ ) ose pla ( __ ) ewt

60 mea ( __ ) ight fil ( __ ) ost

5

Add one letter to the word in capital letters to make a new word. The meaning of the new word is given in the clue.

B 12

| | | | |
|---|---|---|---|
| **Example** | PLAN | simple | plain |
| 61 | ARE | not covered | ______ |
| 62 | MAN | most important | ______ |
| 63 | RAT | a float | ______ |
| 64 | OVER | put on top of | ______ |
| 65 | SORT | little | ______ |

5

***Now go to the Progress Chart to record your score!*** **Total** 65

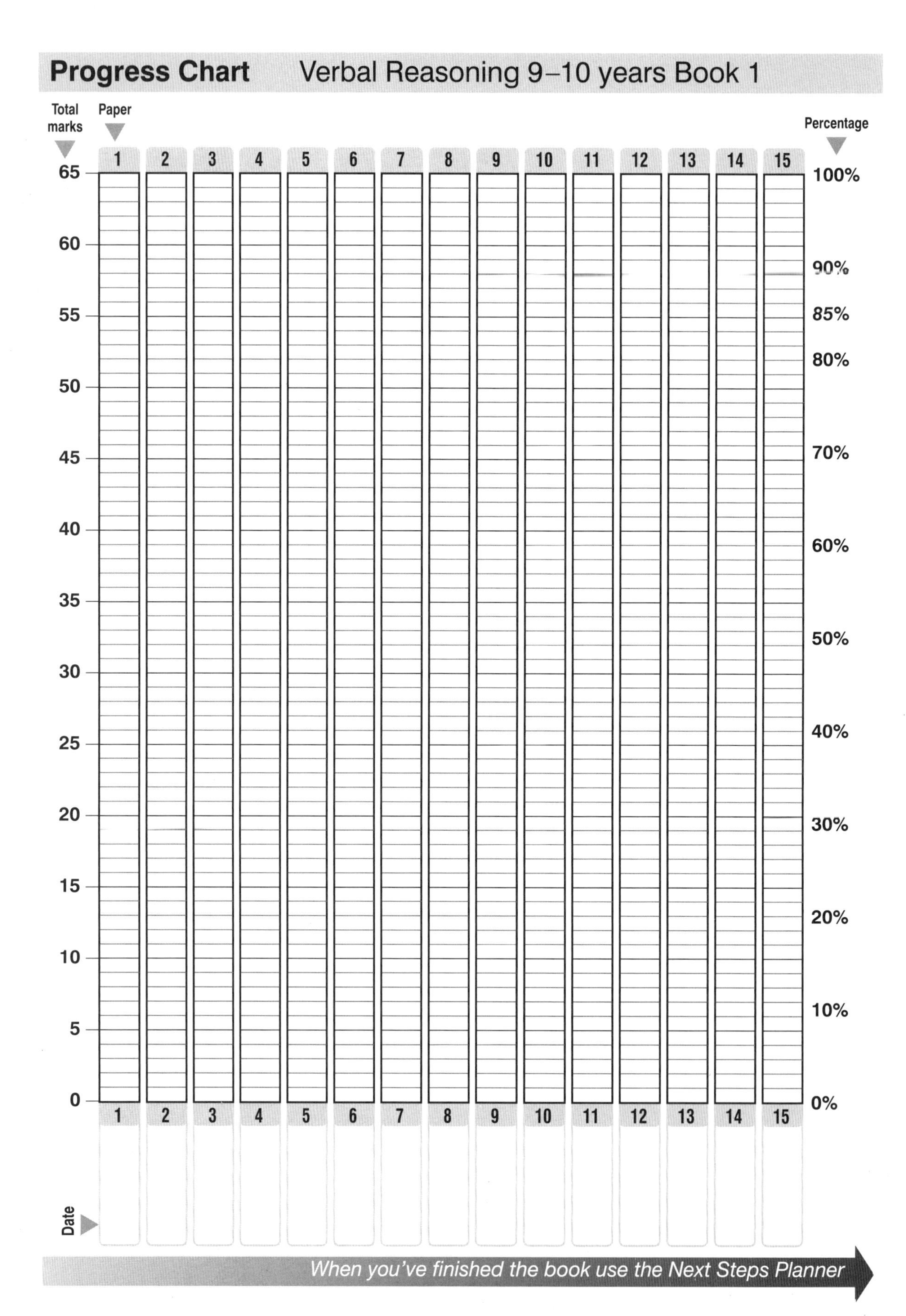
Progress Chart
Verbal Reasoning 9–10 years Book 1
Total marks
Paper
Percentage
1 2 3 4 5 6 7 8 9 10 11 12 13 14 15
65 60 55 50 45 40 35 30 25 20 15 10 5 0
100% 90% 85% 80% 70% 60% 50% 40% 30% 20% 10% 0%
Date
When you've finished the book use the Next Steps Planner